Magnitude 7

The People of
Christchurch,
Canterbury & Beyond
Tell
Their Stories

A time to tear down and a time to build,
a time to weep and a time to laugh,
a time to mourn and a time to dance,
a time to scatter stones and a time to gather them,
a time to embrace and a time to refrain,
a time to search and a time to give up,
a time to keep and a time to throw away,
a time to tear and a time to mend.

Ecclesiastes 3:3-7

Magnitude 7.1 & 6.3

ISBN 978-1469955612

First published in New Zealand in 2011

Dedication

To the people of Christchurch and Canterbury who have lost so much and still greet each day with a smile. To those who are working through the aftermath of the earthquakes and the accompanying emotions. To those who have unshakeable hope that the final result will be a better, stronger city.

Kia kaha Christchurch.

Be strong. You are loved and supported by many.

Foreword

Numbers, dates and times hold significance for us as human beings. Mention 7.1 or 6.3 to a Cantabrian and inevitably their thoughts will go to scenes of devastation and destruction. The same applies to the dates of 4th September 2010, 22nd February 2011, and 13th June 2011. The events of these three days are indelibly seared into the lives of every person who experienced the Christchurch earthquakes – as well as many thousands of people who watched the events unfold on television and through newspapers. This book is a collection of personal stories of how the earthquakes impacted the lives of men, women and children. They tell of their fear, trauma and disbelief. They share feelings of shock, anger, guilt and grief. And most importantly, they reflect the hope and resilience that has caused the people of Christchurch and Canterbury to rise up and begin the process of rebuilding their lives and city.

Contents

Chapter One – Earthquake

September 4th 2010, 4:35am

The bed was moving, banging and shaking, vibrating in the predawn darkness.

The log burner's overheated the water!

Then I realised we no longer had a log burner. It had been replaced by a heat pump five months earlier. I threw the covers back and jumped out of bed. Something was seriously wrong and a surge of adrenaline brought me to instant consciousness. Kevin was already standing by the door and shouted that we needed to get downstairs. Before I could take a single step, however, the bedroom seemed to bend in half, throwing me against the window behind me.

It's an earthquake ... but Christchurch doesn't get earthquakes ... we're supposed to be safe here!

Then my thoughts turned to the children. *We've got to get them out of the house.* The problem was I couldn't move, not even to take one step. The floor was rocking and heaving and I clawed helplessly at the bed as the motion thrust me against the window, over and over.

The house is going to split in half. I'm going to be thrown through the glass to the ground below.

After 40 seconds or so, the motion subsided and I was able to move again. My heart was thumping wildly as Kevin looked across at me. "You're as white as a sheet," he said.

I realised my whole body was shaking and my legs wobbled as I followed him out of the bedroom. Chantelle, our youngest child, met us on the landing and we threw Daniel's door open, calling him to follow us. The house was still shuddering, banging and shaking as we stumbled downstairs and stopped at Tim's room to call him. Kirstin met us in the passage, wide-eyed and excited. "How cool was that!" Noel, who lives with us, had gone next door to the church to shut off the alarm and see if anything was damaged.

We congregated in the lounge, stunned and shocked, looking at each other, offering a few comments about what had just happened. Coming from Africa, we had no idea about earthquakes or what they felt like. All we knew was that Christchurch was not supposed to be on a fault line. I remember thinking the quake couldn't have been too bad as our lights were still working. However, a strong aftershock struck a few minutes later and we were left in darkness. No one knew where a torch was and I scratched around for a few tea-light candles. We arranged these on the kitchen counter and the dim light cast flickering shadows across the room.

I hope they won't set fire to the house if we have another large shake.

An hour later, after a brief visit from our young neighbour, the family drifted back to bed one by one. I lingered to inspect the damage by the pale light of dawn. We'd left the washing up water in the sink the night before and the force of the quake had spread it across the kitchen floor. A metre-tall speaker was on its face, books had toppled, cupboards had been flung open, creams, perfumes, photos and ornaments had fallen – but miraculously nothing inside the house was broken. Outside, the low wall on the side of our veranda had broken in two. The joint where the garage joined the house was cracked and two panels of the garage roof had twisted and split - but there was no serious damage.

Thank you God for protecting us.

I went upstairs to join Kevin, still feeling shaky and shocked. "We'd better text family in South Africa," I said as I climbed into bed. "I've a feeling this might make it onto their news." As I started sending messages, texts came in from Jason and Erin, our son and daughter-in-law, and from friends in other parts of New Zealand. *Are you alright? Is anything damaged? Was everyone home when it happened?*

Just before 6am, I got out of bed again. "I can't just lie here," I said to Kevin. "I want to know what's happening." With no power and no battery-operated radios in the house, I had to sit in the car to listen to the news. The earthquake took up the entire 6am broadcast and reports talked of damaged roads, burst water pipes and facades falling off buildings in the city centre. The magnitude was reported as a 7.1.

My journalistic instincts kicked in and I rushed back inside. "I'm going into town. I need to see what's happened." I knew instinctively that this was an event worth recording; a once in a lifetime chance to see the devastation wrought by the force of nature.

3

By this time, Kevin was up as well. "I'm going into work to see if everything's alright there."

As I was about to leave, Chantelle, 15, appeared in her pyjamas. "I want to come with you." Normally she wouldn't leave the house in her pyjamas ... but this wasn't a normal day by any standards. "We'll go past Dad's work on the way," I told her. Kevin works as a mechanic for Ritchies Transport, a company that owns and operates bus services around New Zealand. He was standing with some work mates, surveying the damage in the workshop. Several metal shelving units had toppled over and lay bent and crushed, strewn with gaskets, lenses and O rings. Thousands of nuts, bolts and spare parts were scattered like metal confetti amongst the wreckage. Chuckles, Kevin's foreman, told us how his chimney had collapsed during the quake. He lives in a two-storey home and the chimney ran the height of the building. When it fell, it ripped the side of the house open, leaving it exposed to the elements.

When he finished his story, it was coming up to 7am. "Come on," I said to Chantelle. "Let's go into town. I'm wondering if they haven't closed the roads off already." As I drove, I noticed how quiet the suburbs were. Few vehicles were on the roads and all the stores were closed. Traffic lights were not working and the radio informed us the airport had been closed and evacuated. The enormity of the situation was slowly working its way into my consciousness.

This is big. This is very big.

As I drove into the CBD, the first building I saw was the Knox Presbyterian Church on Bealey Ave. It was surrounded by chunks of masonry and had lost brickwork from its gables. The damage to a row of shops opposite the church was more severe. The building had lost the entire frontage from the upper floor, and the ground in front of it was a massive pile of bricks, topped with several window frames. Walls are a protection against the world and when they fall, the things they hide are exposed for the world to see. It felt obscene and wrong; like we were peering into places that were private. A few people clustered at the emergency tape, and I joined them, taking photographs of the damage and staring at the upper rooms. There was little in the way of conversation and people's faces echoed the shock and disbelief I was feeling.

From there, I drove as far into the centre of the city as I could and my pyjama-clad daughter and I spent the next hour walking around the CBD. On a Saturday morning, Christchurch central normally buzzes. Trams run, buses rumble in and out of the Bus Exchange and people socialise at dozens of coffee shops. On this Saturday, there was an eerie calm. Few cars were around, no buses, no stores were open, no planes overhead. Just this terrible scene of destruction. It was intensely emotional knowing the skyline of our city had been irrevocably changed; that people's dreams and livelihoods had been shattered in less than a minute.

Familiar buildings had sustained severe damage and piles of rubble lay everywhere. I paused on Manchester Street and took a series of photos of the remains of Westende Jewellers.

The facade had collapsed and a restaurant on the first storey lay exposed for all to see. Incredibly, the tables and chairs were still in position although walls on two sides were gone. On Madras Street I paused to examine a gold-coloured BMW that had been crushed by falling bricks. Then I realised Kevin and I had walked through that exact area the night before. We'd been to a 21st party at the Twisted Hop and had come out and crossed the street exactly where the bricks lay.

If the earthquake had happened six hours earlier, we might have been buried under the rubble!

As Chantelle and I walked around, frequent aftershocks shook the city and people instinctively moved away from crumbling buildings. Police and emergency workers were scattered around, cordoning off areas and warning the public to stay back. One of these areas was the surrounds of Manchester Courts. This seven-storey red brick building suffered extensive cracking and structural damage in the earthquake and was visibly unsafe. As I gazed around, taking in the damage around me, it was surreal, like a scene from a movie.

This can't be happening. It's a bad dream.

After taking dozens of photos, Chantelle and I returned to the car and drove through another section of the CBD before taking a circuitous route home. As I drove, I noticed pockets of damage everywhere I looked. Manhole covers and shafts had been pushed out of roads, tarmac was rippled and cracked, chimneys and garden walls had collapsed, entire suburban shopping malls lay in ruins and silt had pushed through the ground, causing flooding and layers of mud. I was absolutely numb.

Could an earthquake of less than a minute really cause this much damage?

I listened to the radio as I drove and updates informed us that almost the entire city was without power. The airport was still closed and Telecom estimated that they had a couple of hours of battery life left before the network in Christchurch would die. The best news was that no deaths had been reported although the hospital was flooded with injuries. Experts said if the earthquake had happened earlier or later, hundreds would probably have died because the streets would have been crowded with people.

Our area was one of the first to have its power restored – about six hours after the earthquake. After loading some photos on to Facebook, I decided to drive to our suburban supermarket on the off chance that I could get some milk. The store was open but it certainly wasn't business as usual. The staff had cordoned off the shelving units and a small section at the front of the store displayed baskets of bread and bottles of milk. Customers were being allowed in a few at a time. After picking up some bread and milk, I moved over to the cordoned-off areas and took pictures of the devastation.

The alcohol section was flooded with wine and beer – a sea of pink, studded with glass and soggy boxes. The floors of the food aisles could hardly be seen as canned goods, fizzy drinks, cosmetics and sauce bottles lay jumbled together. Members of the public worked side by side with staff to clean up the mess.

The rest of the day was spent in a haze, chatting on Facebook, texting friends and watching earthquake footage on TV. One of the channels had set up full coverage and we saw railway tracks twisted like spaghetti, the rift where the earth had lifted along the fault line, boundary fences displaced by three metres, homes split in two, buildings sitting at alarming angles and silos crushed and collapsed.

As I had anticipated, the city centre was cordoned off shortly after I left it but television cameras were allowed in to relay the damage to the world. We watched as a fire broke out on Worcester St. The building affected was next door to the city office of Ritchies transport and was caused by a gas leak. The gas caught fire when power was restored to the city.

The earth beneath my feet had always been something I trusted: a secure place to stand and a safe place to build upon. Along with 400,000 people in the Christchurch region, that security was shattered in less than a minute. As I went to bed that night, aftershocks continued to rattle the house, echoing the emotions that churned within. I felt shocked, insecure and vulnerable. News reports had warned of a possible large aftershock and I was afraid I would be awoken by another major earthquake during the night. I had no idea of what my beloved city was about to be plunged into over the following months.

Chapter Two – What Just Happened?

The 4th September earthquake came as a terrible shock to the people of Christchurch and Canterbury. Most people were asleep at the time and awoke to homes and buildings that were banging, rocking and lurching in every direction. As the shaking stopped, people reacted in different ways. Families gathered, friends phoned, texts were sent, neighbours checked on each other and emergency personnel responded.

Within minutes, most people realised how poorly prepared they were for a natural disaster. With the power off, they were left scratching in the dark for torches, candles and matches. Some had battery-operated radios and others went and sat in cars to listen to news updates. Still others sat in their gardens, too scared to re-enter damaged properties. In the CBD, shocked guests were evacuated from hotels. The following stories reflect some of the emotions experienced as the 4th September unfolded.

Childhood Innocence by Shirley Shelton

It sounded like a speeding, fully-laden freight train invading my home. Horrendously, terrifyingly loud, it was accompanied by violent shaking: earthquake!

My first thought was for my two granddaughters in the next room. Once out of bed, I was immediately thrown against the window and then the floor. I clawed my way along the bed and covered my nakedness with my dressing gown. The lights went out. I felt for my daughter, Rachel, in the girls' room. She'd plucked 20-month-old Georgia out of her cot and pulled three-year-old Millie, still in her little nest of large cushions and duvets away from the window. She sat on the floor cuddling her little girls. I bounced off the hall walls on the way to the lounge to find my husband. Suddenly, the invasion stopped.

In the contrasting silence and stillness, I found Richard holding onto the lounge wall. Rachel, her seventeen-year-old daughter Olivia, Millie and Georgia came into the lounge. No one said anything. Frantic rattling from the flue in the newly installed log burner heralded another loud, jolting quake. I froze. We all stood still, huge scared eyes searching scared eyes for reassurance. Will it stop?

We had no power or water. Using torchlight, we lit candles, took pictures off walls and put stored water on the log burner to boil. We listened to the battery-powered radio. "At 4:35am, Saturday the 4th September 2010, an earthquake occurred on an unknown fault line, at a depth of 10 kilometres. The epicentre was the farming community of Darfield, 40 kilometres southwest of Christchurch. It lasted 30 seconds and measured 7.1 on the Richter scale." Terrified voices from every quarter of the Canterbury region described their experiences.

The frequent aftershocks were frightening. I tried not to react because of my grandchildren. I must've succeeded because Millie, cuddled in a duvet on my knee looked at the candles and the fire, then looked up at me. "Nana, this is so much fun," she said.

Tears must've been closer to the surface than I thought. Several leaked down my cheek. I hid my head in the duvet protecting my precious bundle. I couldn't talk. It was three days later when I told the family what Millie had said.

The earthquake was the longest 30-second period of my life. I've never been so scared or felt so helpless. Two weeks and over 700 aftershocks later, every Cantabrian had lost something but miraculously no-one lost anybody. My home wasn't damaged.

The damage was in my head. I was nervous and with every creak in the house I tensed up. I was so apprehensive that I found myself reluctant go to bed at night. I enjoyed driving my taxi because I had respite from the day-time aftershocks. A down-side to taxi driving was that I saw the devastation wreaked on the buildings. My problems were minuscule compared to the tired, haunted, bewildered faces of people in the worst-hit areas who were, and are the real legacy of this catastrophe.

Freight Train Experience by Ruth Davey

Wow! What a way to wake up! At 4:35 this morning, I woke up to a sound like a freight train passing very close to the house, and then suddenly it was like I was in a carriage of the freight train. Everything was shifting and rocking; I could hear the frame of the house stretching and shifting and the entire bed swayed, just like a train going round a bend. I opened my eyes and it was pitch black. What was happening? And then I realised – I'm living in an earthquake zone and this is an earthquake - the real deal!

So I dove out of bed to try to get to the door frame to stand under it. My daughter, Hannah, said she worked out what was going on and decided she was as safe in bed - she put her pillows over her head in case anything fell on her. My son, Paul, was working on his laptop and just sat there, in bed, shell-shocked, waiting for it to pass. He said it was an interesting experience.

The shaking lasted for about 30 seconds to a minute - way worse than the Johannesburg earth tremors from the blasting in the mines. It also seemed much longer. This was a 7.1 quake on the Richter scale. Not a fun experience or one I would like to repeat again.

I was wide awake by now. The house stopped rocking and I looked around to see what damage there was. Only one bookcase fell over - books everywhere in the passageway. Some cupboard doors shook open, but nothing else fell down. The lights lasted long enough for me to see all that, then it went dark. Electricity was out for about six hours. The poor cat was so traumatised she refused to come inside. She didn't even have a proper breakfast - too scared to eat. She thought it was safer to sit outside, even if it was cold.

The family and I moved all the books into piles on the floor in the lounge and dismantled the book shelf. Then we went back to bed to keep warm and wait for first light. Sleep? You must be joking! And no morning cup of tea either. But we did have water.

When it was light my husband, Gordon, managed to get the side door of the garage open. The main door is electric - no good hoping that would open until the electricity was on again. There he got the gas bottles and the camp stove and kettle and we had a good cup of tea. I found a battery-operated radio and some torches in the dark, but mostly we just needed to wait for the light. Our area got off lightly. In the centre of town some building fronts fell down and in Avonside, which is built on sand, the roads were damaged - huge cracks and sand and water pushed up through them. Some houses had chimneys fall down. In Kaiapoi it looks like the Kaiapoi River jumped its banks during the quake and flooded the streets of the town.

Okay, so I've done my earthquake now. No more please.

Wake Up Call by The Visser Family

On the morning of 4 September 2010 sometime round about 4:30am the earth shook me and said it's time to wake up. I can only remember certain points, like getting out of bed with Angelique already in my arms. The Lord sent her to our bed sometime in the wee hours of that morning. I remember looking to my right and seeing Caren catching a mirror as it came crashing down. She did a good job and it didn't break. We didn't speak as we jumped out of bed. The sound was tremendous, a cacophony. I don't think we realized at that stage what was going on, but survival instinct kicked in and we headed for the door.

Caren later recalled seeing toilet water splashing on the floor, and somewhere between the bedroom and the front door we lost all electric power. It felt like the walls from the hallway were swinging so much that that they touched us, first the left one, then the right. Running through the living area, we saw CD's lying on the floor. We can't recall who opened the door, but I remember kneeling down, trying to get rid of the sudden rush of blood to the brain.

After talking to the neighbours we sat under blankets on the front porch for about half an hour. When we finally made the decision to return inside, Angelique went back to bed. We were kept awake by the constant aftershocks. It was only after power was restored that we saw the images of our beloved Christchurch and realized that all the prayers for protection had paid off.

Earthquake blues by Elizabeth Robertson

Once the writhing walls had been blanked
out by the loss of light we were in the dark
belly of a moving monster that heaved
us around at its will trying to devour us we lay
stunned in our beds that had now betrayed us
and were no longer safe, stable, so that we
could never quite trust them again.

An evil bouncy castle imprisoned us inside
its suffocating skin of terror and helplessness
was the most appalling part we all endured
when we rushed outside and sat shivering
on the lawn and the paving in our treacherous
gardens which let grey sticky innards ooze
up and envelope us the unwary victims.

Stairs swayed and the lamps cracked apart
and so glass gleefully slashed unfettered
at our cold feet unshod and unsafe
and the easterly wind tore at thin night
wear and his nude body, when night wear
was once an option but no longer and doors
remain unlocked

throughout the night and burglars and
potential murders now come a close

18

second to aftershocks that could smother
and cover us with dusty debris and slabs
of death that look like white chocolate
splintered, deadly, crushing us down
to sleep with the demons who

rise up from the spirit world where Tantalus
begs for a drop of water in Hades and we
would have to be as strong as Sisyphus,
lifting, a hopeless quest so we rush outside
or crouch under fragile tables and stand
in splintered doorways clutching murky
water bottles in fading torchlight
just in case.

A Rock 'n Roll Experience by Dawn Eagle – Part One

Friday 3rd September 2010 was an unprepossessing
day which ended the same way as usual, turning the
bedside light out about midnight and dropping off to sleep.
However, what happened next changed my life forever. At
4.35am on Saturday 4th September I was woken very
suddenly with an extremely loud noise and unbelievable
vibration and movement. My only thought was that there
had been an air accident and a plane had smashed through
the roof.

The noise and movement went on for about 15
seconds, then eased off slightly, which made me realise it
was a very strong earthquake, not an air crash. The lights
flickered and went off, and I was paralyzed with fear when
the noise and movement started again, working up to
another frenzy. The earthquake eased off a little before

intensifying again several times - in truth it was less than a minute in total, but when lying petrified in bed in complete darkness, time stood still. If my life had depended on it I could not have jumped out of bed and stood in a doorway in the approved fashion.

My heart was beating so fast it seemed to leap out of my chest, and I was welded to the bed too afraid to take a deep breath in case it all started up again. The ground rumbled as though a freight train was close, and the bed moved up and down and side to side like a boat in rough seas. What should I do? My bedroom is upstairs, and there was no-one near to help – no point in calling out to anyone. The noise of the quake had been so loud I hadn't realized that everything had been thrown off my bedside table and tallboy and the floor was littered with the detritus which accumulates in a personal space.

My cell phone rang and I tentatively put my hand down to find the torch which was always kept beside the bed. I answered it with a very tentative, "Hello." It was my son Andrew. He asked if I was alright and I burst into tears. He said he'd be down soon so I made myself get out of bed, find my dressing gown and put on my sneakers, the most sensible decision I made that morning. I tentatively made my way down the stairs, holding onto the railing very tightly as the house was still moving. On the landing my large vase had been overturned, blocking the way, the first sign of the damage that I would find through the house.

Downstairs, into the kitchen. The china cabinet doors were open and many things had been flung onto the floor. I was thankful that I had my sneakers on, as every step crunched through broken wine glasses, fancy china, and precious ornaments. I didn't stop, making my way to the door to unlock it for Andrew, and watched the best sight in the world, a wavering torchlight coming up the driveway.

Andrew brought two candles with him and he lit these, leaving me in the sunroom while he went to the garage to let Josh, my border collie out. Poor Josh, he was as scared as we were. The shakes and loud rumbling noises were practically continuous, and all we could do was sit numbly and wait for the dawn light, both of us trembling with shock and cold as frost was settling on the ground and without power there was no way of heating the room. I wrapped a blanket around my shoulders, and so we sat, two humans and one dog, scared and cold, waiting for the first light.

As the sky lightened in the east the birds started singing, the first small sign of normality, and as the darkness faded we walked around the house between tremors. All my clothes were upstairs and I was very scared to go there in case there were further strong quakes, but I knew I had to get fully dressed to get warm. It was then that I found the damage in my bedroom. Every earring had come off the stand, my rings were all over the floor, video tapes were all across the room, and in the en suite, every bottle of perfume had landed in the basin.

As soon as it was light enough Andrew walked around my house to check for damage, and thankfully, apart from the log fire chimney being a bit twisted there was no obvious damage outside. So he lit the fire to warm the house and us up. With no power there was also no water but we were able to get some water from the hot tap as we both felt the need for a hot drink.

Andrew said he'd go down to his house and bring back his camping cooker, but I was very reluctant to let him go. My nerves were so frazzled I was scared to be alone for even a few minutes, but I could see the sense in it so I sat in the sunroom watching him, not daring to move.

After a hot drink things looked a little brighter, and with the sun coming through we picked up the worst of the broken glass before Josh cut his paws on it. It was heartbreaking – all that was left of my late mother's coffee set was one cup and two saucers. The broken cups and saucers could possibly be replaced, but I don't want to do that. They were precious because my mother had treasured them, and any replacements would be just that - replacements. They wouldn't be the cups which she had carefully washed, held and displayed, so it would be better to just keep the survivors and the memories.

Prayer by Robert Simpson

Dear Lord Jesus,

We are so thankful that we have been saved from the 7.1 earthquake that struck this city at 4.35 on Saturday morning, the 4th September, 2010.

We are full of praise.

We are thankful that we have been able to take succeeding aftershocks in our stride, even though we have not welcomed any of them.

We rejoice in this, the small things of survival. We are thankful too, that in spite of the sounds of hands scrabbling outside the bedroom wall with absolute cruelty, they didn't get in.

We are full of praise.

We are thankful as well for the extensive books, bookcases, pictures, wall paintings and Bibles were laid on the bed so neatly that on waking, God must be thanked as we see the confusing mess.

We praise your Name.

We are thankful for the welcome friends and neighbours, the mayor and Prime Minister, radio, TV and newspapers, all telling us, in measured tones, keep calm: help is on its way.

We are full of praise.

We are thankful that in spite of the precious objects of art and lovely statues being destroyed, the enormous painting has just slithered down, and the massive new TV has been saved!

We are full of praise.

We are thankful, that in most cases, the churches in Canterbury have not fallen down, so we can praise your name, always!

Wake Up Call by Kay Graham – Part One

"See you later, love. Catch lots of fish," I mumbled, rolling over and burying my head under the covers. I was asleep again before the garage door went down behind my husband's truck.

I woke to a massive creaking and groaning sound, and the feel of the bed heaving under me like a ship on the sea. In a moment I was up and racing down the hall to my daughter's room. "Come under the doorway Miri, it's an earthquake!"

She told me later that I pulled her out of bed and under the door frame, but I don't remember it. Just hanging onto the frame with one hand and clutching her to me with the other, trying to keep us both on our feet. And then the lights went out.

In the darkness and sudden quiet, I focused on the sound of a door squeaking as it swung backwards and forwards on its hinges. It seemed to go on forever, though it could only have been a moment before the lights came back on and the shaking began again. When it finally stopped, we stayed where we were for a while, just holding onto one another. I remember being relieved it was over, but that was the only feeling I had. Miriama was in the same condition I think. When I suggested we check how much damage had been done, she had no qualms about letting go of me, and in fact she led the way up to the lounge.

Looking back, I'm amazed how tidy the house still was. All the smaller ornaments on the wall unit had fallen over on the shelves or onto the floor, but my 65 cm china doll was still standing and my books were intact. Miri's books, though, were all over the floor, covered in water from the fish tank, whilst Miri's fish, Boo, darted around in 2/3 of a tank of water. That was the worst damage we had.

Miri and Boo were alright, but I couldn't do anything about finding the rest of the family. There was no sign of our three cats; if we had taken torches to check on the guinea pigs, they would have been more scared than ever; and my husband didn't have a cell phone. He could already have been fishing in Lake Pearson for all I knew.

I was beginning to worry about the missing ones, and it was a relief when Casper and Jemima hopped in through the cat flap. Even better, the garage door went up shortly afterwards, when my husband Ian returned home. I had to wait another hour, though, before my beautiful big tabby cat, Tigger, crawled out from under our bed, giving a subdued version of his musical greeting.

By then, we had cleaned up the water and climbed back into bed. Our bed – all of us. Ian and I on the outside, Miri and her cat Casper in the middle, and Ian's cat Jemima on his feet. Tigger joined us there, and after a brief complaint from Jemima – his sister – we all settled down again.

It was a shock to tune into a radio station and hear how much damage had been done in Canterbury. That was when the reality of what had happened hit me, and I couldn't stop crying. Some of my tears were sheer relief, because I realised Ian and his friends had had a lucky escape. They normally left to go fishing at around 2.30am but because John was ill, Ian and Malcolm had opted to leave two hours later, and were still in Woodend when the earthquake hit. Otherwise they would have been on the banks of the lake, or even up to their chests in the water. I firmly believe God was looking out for them that night.

Earthquake by Allan Horwell

Silence

Just before birdsong

It strikes

The subterranean

soil-splicer is full-blown

and nasty

As a consequence

You're wrenched from slumber

Your heartbeat soars

Grasped by a shudder

Of wreck force intensity

You're flashed by the thought

Of death by quake

The crazy house

Lurches and sways

on an imagined precipice

Objects tumble, smash

You totter along the hall

Into the dining room

You switch on the radio

A strew of objects covers the floor space

Wall pictures are skewed

Ceiling lights sway

Caught in surreal ambience

In anticipation

You tug chairs from the dining table

Weep, feel nauseous

Beyond, there's an assortment of voices

Relieved, you join survivors

thrush sings

New day begins

Chapter Three – Day One Unfolds

Police and emergency workers were on the scene in Christchurch central within minutes of the earthquake, assessing damage and cordoning off affected buildings. As dawn broke, the number of people walking the streets increased. Many had cameras in hand and all had expressions of disbelief and shock as they photographed buildings with collapsed facades, crushed cars, and roads with deep crevasses in them. Police shouted warnings as they set up barriers and asked the public to move back. Frequent aftershocks added to the fear as buildings groaned and shook, cascading showers of cement and dust. At this stage, many people had not realised what a large area the earthquake had affected.

Working on Earthquake Damage by Isaac Noble

The morning of the 4th September my wife, Hannah, shook me awake in alarm as our caravan swayed and shook. At first I thought it might be some partygoers giving it a push but then realised it was an earthquake. The caravan absorbed some of the motion so I only found out later how big it had been.

I work for Fulton Hogan and at 8am I got an urgent call to go into the city centre. By 9am I was manning a road block as the police secured the CBD. There were a lot of people wanting to get into town to see the damage and some were quite abusive. I found that stressful and it was a relief to get back to what I'm employed to do. By the afternoon I was operating a 5-ton digger in town, clearing the rubble from collapsed buildings.

It was a really big shock to see the extent of the damage. To begin with we were loading the rubble onto trucks for dumping. Then the building engineers asked us to simply push it to the sides as they were worried one of the frequent aftershocks would bring more buildings down. We worked a lot faster after that!

Over the next few days, I was sent to a number of different areas and some memories stand out clearly. Although I was shocked at the damage the earthquake had wrought, it was the emotions of people that got to me. We spent some time on Seabreeze Close in Bexley and I was dumbfounded at the amount of liquefaction the area had experienced. The street was swamped with silt that spread from side path to side path, completely covering the street. We sat at smoko time and looked at the way the houses were sitting at angles and how some had sunk into the ground. People's driveways and gardens were also full of silt but we were told we could only clear the road area. An elderly man approached me and asked if I could clear his driveway so he could get his caravan out. I told him we were not allowed to and he broke down in tears. I went back a little later and the council allowed us to clear driveways.

Later in the week, I was driving a digger on a truck through Halswell towards Akaroa. I was doing 90kmh when I hit a bridge that had lifted by about 15 centimetres. The road was full of ripples and corrugations and I was amazed at the damage.

Before the September earthquake, I had experienced a couple of minor tremors in the Nelson area but nothing big like the Christchurch earthquake. The physical damage is manageable, but the emotional damage could be endless.

Drama in Hororata by Carol Gurney

Our home is a genuine piece of NZ paradise. We pulled down the old cottage about 10 years ago which was the original cool house to the Hororata homestead. They knew a thing or two about building sites but ours is the best, nestled amongst mature trees, overlooking an unnamed stream which starts from behind Allan's place just across the road. It has mud fish, but I haven't seen a trout in years. The ducks, pukekos, kingfishers, shags and our dogs love it. We have 14 bright-red gold fish from the lake down at the domain that are having a holiday here as the lake is being repaired.

Our home is made from macracarbe, bagged brick and shingles, two storeys overlooking our 15 acres and the three rivers. The Hororata is our boundary ... paradise...

31

What is that noise! It's so loud I'm awake but can't determine what's happening. Then I feel the bed shaking wildly, bloody dogs, Olive snoring. What is that noise, what's shaking me and throwing me out of bed on to the floor? I can't stand up, Olive can't hear me, noise all around. Quick, get to the door frame, it's an earthquake! I still can't see and the two huge wooden sideboards have fallen at the head of the bed so I clamber over these and meet Olive in the door well. Two naked, fat ladies over 55 sharing an average-sized door well is a very tight fit. Add to that equation a corgi and a border terrier under my chin. We are telling each other we are okay, it's over , breathing hard, asking what the f*** happened and oh my god here we go again. We're still in darkness and the shaking was more like a huge boat going from side to side, up and down. Thought the roof would give in this time and was prepared to die with my beautiful wife beside me. I promised to be a better listener and not so impatient. Harrison – pissed off I won't see my grandson grow into the incredible man he will be, thank god my daughter, Corrin has a wonderful man to support her in her time of sorrow.

Then it stopped. We are alive but exhausted. I can't remember the sounds but we needed to get out of the house NOW. In the dark we got Crocs and dressing gowns and a torch. We made our way downstairs, climbing over things large and small. At the end of the stairs is the door to the kitchen, which couldn't be opened –straight out the back door. We are both shaking, using the lord's name in vain over and over. It's really cold with a good frost so we jump in the truck and turn it on so we can use the heater. I notice our neighbour's hazard lights on and point this out to Olive who can't see a thing as her glasses are in the house. Off I go inside - up the stairs –thank god for my Crocs, stuff everywhere, scrambling over things and go straight to the floor in front of where the glasses are normally kept for the night. Yippee! Down the stairs, crying now as I see the broken mess.

We drive over the road in our truck to be met by Allan our neighbour. He is a fast mover and talker at the best of times. The man is manic - his son has been thrown out of the top storey of their house, a very English two-storey, triple red brick, and landed by the new Mercedes followed by the rest of the top storey. He's not dead but covered in dust, moaning in shock. Allan insists on driving us back down his drive to show us his house. It looks like a huge bomb has landed as one side of the house is just not there. I start to cry and just want to see if our friends and family are okay. Back down the drive to wait for the ambulance that Allan has called. We get Allan to drive us across the road to our place to get blankets and pillows as Xavier is in shock, moaning, scared and looking very pale under all the dust. The ambulance arrives and we have a quick word about what's happening. The guys shake their heads and say it's not good, Christchurch is a mess.

Up the road to another neighbour - Patterson Parkin, the artist and his partner, Sue, who we find sitting with the heater on in their truck. They say all their contents are on the floor and broken. They aren't going anywhere until daylight. Looking like frightened little possums we leave them and move down the road to our elderly neighbours. As we approach the Hororata bridge we see that both sides have risen about two feet, just where the land meets the bridge.

Noelene and Bill, both in their 80's, are in the bedroom as we call out and make our way down the hall, climbing over mountains of stuff. They are still shaking and said other neighbours had already been and they also were going to stay in bed.

We don't notice the St. John's church and as we pass our cafe it looks intact. Vic and Nic not home and the window is open-are they in hospital? Are they okay? Up the road to Chris and Merv. Hugs, crying, talking, tea off the fire, people calling in, Jane and Peter are in a state, their house to come down soon.

Sorry I can't do this.

My cafe and wine bar is a mess with eight fridges' contents on the floor. Booze, glasses, food all over the place. We go into the cafe, shake our heads and go home for lunch-which we get off the floor. It is wrapped with a few salvaged bottles of wine. When we get back Steve and Nic have been hard at it and have cleared so much

Later all these dear friends get together and we clean and clear for days. Three large wheelie bins of broken preserves from Vicki's pantry. We shovel for hours and work in shifts as the fumes are hard on the senses – love these people.

Legless Elves by Lois Farrow

"It's an earthquake," we say in unison as the bed rocks and rolls beneath us. I lie still, eyes wide open in the dark. *The ceiling isn't falling down, the walls aren't falling in, we're okay, this is probably the biggest earthquake I've felt, the ceiling's not falling, we're okay, how long will this go on, when will it stop?*

It stops. Whew!

In the spare bedroom the grandsons, five and seven, are awake but calm, they have no idea what happened.

On the nearby street the boys' parents race to the boys' bedrooms to find the beds empty. Perhaps the toilet? No child! Of course! They are at Mum and Dad's. A few texts back and forth reassure us that we are all okay.

My husband goes outside. In our brand new street, we know of only two occupied houses nearby. The neighbours are okay. (Weeks later we learned that a single lady, moved in the week before, was so traumatised she could not sleep in her house for three months.)We pile into our bed with the children and a wind-up radio and wait for daylight.

We have no power, but we do have water. When daylight comes, we get dressed and survey the minor damage. In the pantry, serviettes and paper plates have fallen from the top shelf, and while two salt shakers have smashed on the floor, the two peppers remain. Ornaments in the wall unit have jammed in the door. Little elves from the wall unit shelf lie legless and although I search I can't find the missing legs. We make do with Weetbix and cold milk for breakfast, and the boys get happily distracted with blocks and cars. Aftershocks continue, and soon the five year old is running up the passage calling, "There's another one, Nana!" Their father comes to collect them.

We walk to the nearby shop to buy the morning paper. People are out on the footpath; conversation is easy as we compare notes. Closer to Halswell we find the sand volcanoes we've heard about on the radio; little mounds of sand pushed up from beneath the footpaths and front lawns. On the way home, we divert to see damage on the road and rising mounds on the once-flat roadside grass.

When we get home it is surreal to read the very ordinary paper (printed during the night) while being part of the unfolding news.

My brother rings from Auckland and holds his phone by the TV so we can hear commentary, although we can't see pictures. We are aghast at the extent of damage in Christchurch. I ring my Wellington brother to let him know we are all right; he had no concern.

"Oh, yes, I felt it, but we're always having little shakes, I didn't know it was a big one." I tell him to watch the news.

Our power comes on in time to watch the evening news; it has been off for twelve hours. Messages come in from overseas. It is comforting to know others are hearing the news and thinking of us.

Okay, so there's been an earthquake but life must go on. The Camellia Society show was already set up in Prebbleton, would we go ahead or not? The local community were planning stalls as well. We shouldn't let them down. All the preparation is done, and the hall is undamaged. We will carry on. Negotiating buckled roads and passing fractured farmland, I drive to Prebbleton. The locals cancel. Too many have damaged houses and are needed at home. Those who do come are glad of company, and happy to delay facing the mess at home.

The following days become a mixture of ordinariness and horror as stories begin to emerge. Having no damage ourselves makes others' stories surreal. We go to help friends with their unspeakable mess. It seems the house has been in a giant shaker, and everything has been tossed around like confetti. A door to an upstairs room can barely be opened to take a peep at computers, desks and books in a jumbled heap. Crates of broken glass, crystal and china line the hallway until insurance assessors can come. Crates of pureed apple mixed with smashed glass are placed outside the back door. We try to vacuum glass from the carpets, while the men refasten fallen garage shelves.

We have friends affected in varying degrees, but our ability to help seems limited. Our church opens as a drop-in centre, and my husband helps with the teams sent around the locality to clear bricks from broken chimneys. We don't go rubber-necking immediately, but after a couple of weeks we go to see damage in the city, and drive to view buckled roads in the country. Only by going to look do we absorb the reality. Only as time goes on do we realise the seriousness of the situation and the extent of the damage.

Unnerving aftershocks continue. My cousin tells of watching the synchronised orchestration of workers in the Postal Centre. Fingers fly as mail is sorted into post boxes. At each aftershock hands freeze mid-air in comical poses, then relax and sorting continues.

Pre-planned events are increasingly cancelled as organisers fear further aftershocks, or are overwhelmed with needs in their homes and communities. It makes me grumpy as I want life to continue as normal, pretend everything is okay, and grasp at group reassurance and comfort.

I don't feel afraid. I reason that if our house wasn't damaged in the big one, the aftershocks shouldn't affect it. But some aftershocks are severe, and people do sustain new damage. Thankfully our new subdivision stands the test, and we and our neighbours are fine. The aftershocks are of varying intensity, and become increasingly wearying and tiresome.

On a weekend out of town I find myself studying the houses we pass in the countryside. How did they fare in the earthquake? Oh, silly me, they didn't have it here.

In the drawers of the wall unit I find the lost legs of the elves. The drawers had swung open in the initial shock, and the legs have nestled among the contents. We'll glue them on one day but not yet; we'll wait till the aftershocks are over.

From a Taxi Driver's Point of View by Dave Palmer

I was one of the lucky ones. When the earthquake struck I was parked in my taxi, waiting for passengers. There was nothing threatening to fall on my head, there was no noise, and the tyres and shock absorbers did their job. I rang home, and my son assured me he and his stay-over friends were okay and the house was not damaged. With that assurance, I stayed out at work.

This has been my first natural disaster. I have often thought about what place God has in these things, having only seen or heard about them from afar.

Very quickly, someone –from Auckland – called talkback and declared the quake to be a judgment from God. I had always wondered about disasters overseas, and whether any of them were judgments from God, and how could you reconcile that with the huge humanitarian efforts that would follow, many in the name of God. Now, I think I understand a little better.

Straight away, people began checking on their neighbours – often meeting them for the first time. People began to share their compassion and skills with each other with no thought of asking for pay. Students and others who may have been out partying were galvanised into action, shovelling tons of silt. And radio stations crackled with hundreds of positive stories from grateful residents. I concluded that I was seeing the mercy of God expressed through people reaching people.

I believe that the Bible is the word of God. In it, Jesus describes such disasters as 'the beginning of birth pangs.' (Matthew ch.24:7-8). To me it is clear that, like other disasters, the earthquake was not in itself a judgment. But it is a very serious and severe warning. Through it,

God asks us all to consider our personal foundation: on what do we place our hope? Through the quake, Jesus is calling us all to place our trust, not on anything on earth, but in Himself, crucified, resurrected and eternal.

Helping with the Big Cleanup by Erin Roome

On the day of the earthquake, my husband Jason and I thought it would be a nice idea to help with the cleanup. I knew that my sister, Robyn, was helping at the Fresh Choice Supermarket where she worked part-time. I sent her a text asking if they needed any extra help and she quickly replied, 'Yes please.'

We arrived at the supermarket and Robyn led us to the aisle where we could help. As we walked behind her, I looked down each aisle at the mess. There was food everywhere and the aisles with sauces and drinks were the worst affected. Robyn put us to work cleaning up the shampoos, soaps and other toiletries. There was a terrible mess, but it did smell quite nice. The floor was very slippery because of all the liquid soap and shampoo so we had to walk very slowly and carefully. There were a couple of other people cleaning up the aisle with us.

We were told to pick up all the fallen over items on the shelves and stand them up in their right place and then sort through the bottles on the floor. Anything broken went into a black rubbish bag. Everything else had to be wiped with a cloth so it was clean and then put back on the shelf. If something was dented or damaged, but not leaking, we had to put it in a trolley so the supermarket could sell it at a discounted price. At first, I tried very carefully not to get dirty, but this proved most difficult. Eventually I gave up and went on my hands and knees on the floor, sorting through and cleaning the items. Once all the items had been removed from the floor we picked up as much of the liquid as we could with paper towels. When we finally finished, the floor looked clean but was still very sticky. A few of the shop workers were going around mopping all the floors.

By the time we had finished cleaning up our aisle most of the other areas had also been done. Because there were so many people helping it didn't take as long as I expected it would. It felt really nice to be able to help someone clean up and both of us were really glad that we offered.

Chapter Four – The Week after the Earthquake

The first week after the September earthquake was a surreal experience for most Christchurch residents. The region rumbled and shook with repeated aftershocks and the city centre was cordoned off and inaccessible to most people. The reality of shattered buildings, broken roads, streets and homes ruined by liquefaction slowly sunk in as people reached out to help each other. A number of welfare centres opened around the city and those with broken homes and fragile nerves were welcomed with open arms. Churches and charities got stuck in and students and volunteers helped serve meals and dig silt. Schools were closed and many businesses were shut as people processed the impact of the earthquake. Some found the aftershocks overwhelming and chose to leave town for a few days to get some sleep and peace of mind. Others felt helpless sitting at home and got involved in any way they could.

Clearing Silt by the Avon River by Hannah Davey

One of my friend's dads was involved with Civil Defence after the earthquake and invited me to go along and help with the clearing up of silt. We worked in the suburbs and spent part of the time in Avonside near the Avon River. When we arrived for duty, there were plenty of people and we divided into smaller groups with a team leader who had a radio. We had to text in and out as a safety precaution due to the ongoing aftershocks and conditions we were working in.

We were not allowed to clear the properties where the homes had been condemned so worked on others in the streets. The silt was really deep in some areas and if I stood on my shovel, it would reach halfway up my gumboots. There were big areas covered in silt and some driveways couldn't even been seen. I shovelled the silt and worked with a person with a wheelbarrow who would wheel a load to the road and tip it out. Some people were using wheelie bins as there weren't enough barrows. It was hard work physically and I had sore muscles, blisters on my hands, and a thick layer of dirt covered me all over by the end of the day.

Many of the people we helped were older and one lady thought my group was her grandchildren who had offered to come and help her clean up. All the people we helped were so appreciative and some offered us cookies, chocolates and drinks while another offered soup. One wanted to pay us and eventually we accepted the $100 and said we would give it to one of the earthquake funds. At lunchtime, we gathered at a school and Dominos came along and distributed a whole lot of free pizzas amongst us.

It was good to be able to help others and great that so many people supported the effort. It showed what people working together can do.

A Rock 'n Roll Experience – Part Two by Dawn Eagle

Andrew insisted that we eat something as the food in the refrigerator and freezer wouldn't last very long. I kept up my liquids, having cups of tea during the day plus a bottle of lemonade which I found in the pantry. When I saw that most of the contents were on the floor I quickly closed the door again.

I asked Andrew to stay with me the first night, as I couldn't face a night on my own with no lights, no television and only a radio for news. The aftershocks were coming at regular intervals, at times every five minutes. He brought his sleeping bag and we both stayed in the lounge where the fire was still going for warmth. I sat in a recliner chair and he tried to sleep on the floor. Life was not normal by any means. Visits to the bathroom were held off as long as possible, as using the toilet when a tremor started was very disconcerting, to say the least.

Josh was very jittery so we let him stay with us too, and he became an early warning system, standing stock-still and pointing towards the east whenever there was to be another shock. About three seconds later the rumbling would start, then after that would be the movement, sometimes a large jolt and sometimes the earth moving in a wave-like motion. Josh was distressed and he tried to get into Andrew's sleeping bag several times during the night.

I was very tired as I'd had only about four hours sleep the night before, but there was no sleep that Saturday night. My whole body trembled violently and I couldn't control it at all. It was the longest night I have ever experienced, and I never want to experience another like it. Being winter it was dark by 6pm and in the dark the rumbling and shaking seemed much worse than in the daytime. By the end of that first 24 hours there had been more than ninety aftershocks, and that was the most unexpected part of the whole experience. You read about strong earthquakes all around the world, but somehow the aftershocks don't get mentioned very much. They can be very strong, as strong as earthquakes, which would make headlines in the evening news if they were individual events, and that first night they were mostly 4 or 5 on the Richter scale.

There were many more aftershocks the next day and I just sat waiting for the next one. With no power, there seemed little else to do. Margaret, a friend of mine, came to visit on Sunday afternoon and invited me to go and stay with her for a few nights. Her home is in an area that didn't seem to be getting the aftershocks quite as badly affected as mine, so I agreed. Unfortunately, it didn't help much as far as sleep is concerned.

By Tuesday, four days after the big one, I knew that I wasn't coping well at all. I went to see my GP and he gave me a few tranquilisers to help me get through the worst, but although I took a pill before going to bed that night I still didn't sleep much more than an hour.

I talked to Andrew on Wednesday and he suggested that as he was working in Nelson on Sunday we could leave on Thursday and drive up the island, stopping off at a couple of places to get away from the aftershocks. I was very grateful for his thoughtfulness and agreed, packing a few dirty clothes as we still had no water and I couldn't do any washing. By this stage that was a mere detail.

As soon as we left on Thursday morning, I felt a huge relief like a weight had lifted off my shoulders and I relaxed for the first time in days. I slept nearly 12 hours that night in a wonderful motel/apartment in Kaikoura, which had two bedrooms, each with its own en suite, plus a lounge and a fully fitted kitchen. To cap it all off, there was also a sea view, and even the rain, which came down in buckets, couldn't stop my overwhelming thankfulness that I was away from Christchurch.

Before we left I had said that I didn't know if I would ever be able to live comfortably in my home again, and that was the way I felt at that time, but after the four days away I felt slightly differently when we arrived back again. The first night back, I decided to sleep upstairs in my bedroom, the first time since the big quake. I picked up a lot of the things which were still all over the floor and it felt pretty much like my usual room, but then nerves took over and I spent nearly the whole night trembling, probably dozing for only an hour or so. There were five shakes overnight, but a worse one came about 9 o'clock on Tuesday morning.

The newspaper kept telling us that the 'experts' were expecting another aftershock of at least 6, which made us all tense up every time the earth moved, in case it was going to be another big one. But it didn't come, thank goodness.

Gradually over the weeks the frequency and intensity lessened, but who would ever have thought that the aftershocks would still be coming three months after the main event. I know I certainly didn't expect that. Now, with more than 3400 under my belt you would think I would be used to them. But no - every time I feel the house shake and hear the rumbling noise my stomach ties itself in knots again and my heart rate goes up. Will life ever be normal again?

Emails from the Quake Zone

From: b.gilbertson
To: erin_gilbie18
Subject: Thinking of you
Date: Sat, 4 Sep 2010 21:26:42 +1200

Saturday, 8am

Erin, I was so relieved to get your text! We got the news at 7 this morning and have been glued to the radio at Dominic's. He got a text from Ruth (his wife) at 4.35am straight after it happened (she's in Chch for some doctor's conference) but he didn't wake us up, just told us when we got up for breakfast. I didn't believe him at first. My god! 7.1!!! that's a hell of a big earthquake. Dominic said that Ruth is ok even though the house she is staying in on the Port Hills had bricks crashing down through the ceiling and it's basically munted. Paul textd me to say he was fine. His place got off pretty lightly. Up here in Blenheim we didn't feel a thing. The stuff they are showing on TV looks horrendous. I'll try phoning Sonada when we get back to Nelson this afternoon. My god, it must have been terrifying!

Love you, Mum

From: b.gilbertson
To: erin_gilbie18
Subject: Thinking of you
Date: Sat, 4 Sep 2010 21:26:42 +1200

Hi Erin.

Saturday, 9am

So good to get your 2nd text. That's incredible that you and Jake managed to meet up with Paul and Amy, and Ingrid and find a place that was serving breakfast! At Ferrymead,

48

of all places! I'm so relieved that you guys all got to be together. Eggs benedict in the middle of an earthquake zone! Amazing!! I've tried your landline a few times but the phone lines are still down. Don't drink any water at all that hasn't been boiled. Thank goodness Sonada is such a modern building and all safe. I'll try ringing you when we get back to Nelson.

Love Mum

From: b.gilbertson
To: erin_gilbie18
Subject: Thinking of you
Date: Sat, 4 Sep 2010 21:26:42 +1200

Sat 3pm. Ok, we're back home now. The news said the phones are still down so guess you're not going to get this Email but so good to know your power is back on. Anyway, hope you are ok and have got enough food in the flat and enough water ... don't use tap water to brush your teeth, use boiled water. This must be so stressful for you. I checked the D&A website for info on the status of the building but their server is down. So, looks like you may have a few days off ahead. The central city sounds like it had some really bad damage, so don't try going in, promise.

Love you. Mum

From: b.gilbertson
To: erin_gilbie18
Subject: Thinking of you
Date: Sun, 5 Sep 2010 21:26:42 +1200

Hi Erin,

Today it's cold and overcast. We've got the fire on. I'm thinking of you and hope you are ok. They reckon the phones will be back on later today so I'll try phoning you at Sonada. There's some pretty incredible stories coming out on TV. I can't believe this is all going on 400 kms away, and we aren't feeling a thing. I wish there was some way I could talk to you.
Love Mum
Ps: hope you are getting enough sleep with all these aftershocks going on. They sound horrendous. Up here we don't feel any of them. This is surreal!

From: erin_gilbie18
To: b.gilbertson
Subject: Thinking of you
Date: Mon, 6 Sep 2010 21:26:42 +1200

Yeah, had a shower and an early night last night - doing nothing all day is quite exhausting! lol. Today me and Jake went out to Kaiapoi - yeah, I know, they hate the sight seers, but apparently Jake has some distant relatives there who Jake's mum wanted to make sure were ok (they weren't even home). Anyway it's pretty shaken up out there (haha excuse the pun), most of town still closed - lots of cracks in the roads and damage... and there are port-a-loos on every corner! We took a picnic out to Woodend beach after that but it was pretty cold and grey (the weather, not the picnic).Got internet back now as well - it was funny, the whole time i was like 'grr its so annoying I don't have internet' but then when it came back i was like aww damn, I was actually kinda enjoying being forced to be without.

The two big aftershocks were exciting last night but I didn't take too much notice because I was half asleep. I had to laugh when I heard on the radio this morning that 100 more people went into the shelters when they felt those aftershocks - i think maybe I was just not so affected coz I didn't have bricks falling in around me, but I can't believe how dramatic some people are being about all this - girls from my class on Facebook all like "I can't stop crying... I don't want to sleep alone anymore..." totally creaming it for all its worth. There was a thing on the news about the trauma this may cause to children – it's only

51

gonna cause them trauma if you tell them that they're
supposed to be traumatized.
Better get to dinner,

xoxo Erin

Ps: I don't swallow any water when I brush my teeth!

Wake Up Call by Kay Graham – Part Two

The day following the earthquake was surreal.
Much of it was spent checking on friends and neighbours,
and answering calls from family and friends checking on
us! The only thing I remember clearly about the whole day
is the time we spent in Kaiapoi, helping to dig out some of
the disgustingly thick, smelly goo which is caused by
liquefaction. It was like digging glue, and my arms ached
for days afterwards.

In the days and weeks that followed, my life
gradually returned to some kind of normality. Like many
other people, I grieved for those whose lives wouldn't be
returning to normal anytime soon, but the earthquake itself
took on a dream-like quality. It seemed simultaneously to
have happened a long time ago and only yesterday; to have
changed everything and changed nothing. Then the
aftershock I think of as the Spencerville quake arrived.

It was the first time Miri had been outside in an
aftershock, and she and her friend Grace came tearing into
the house in a panic. To calm them down, I suggested we
look around to see if there had been any damage done to
the house, confident we wouldn't find any. After all, it was
only an aftershock, wasn't it?

It wasn't one of my better ideas – something which became apparent as soon as we discovered the first crack around a doorframe. The girls were at once both scared and wildly excited, and insisted on going round the entire house, pointing out everything that looked as if it could be earthquake damage. I followed them around, writing down what we discovered and feeling sick. Although none of it looked serious, it was still a shock to find our home had been affected. By the time we had finished, I had a long list of minor damage and a headache. Needing to talk to an adult, I rang Miri's Godmother, Joyce. Her company was a blessing, and she stayed with me until Ian came home from work.

I thought carefully before I made a claim to EQC, as the damage obviously wasn't structural. But I knew it would have to be repaired, and I was worried about the condition of the garage wall. Once the claim was made, we were fortunate enough to be dealt with quickly. The assessors were here within a month, and the cheque arrived just after Christmas.

We went on holiday to Kaiteriteri in the New Year, and returned home on the 13th of January. Exactly a week later, there was another strong aftershock. Feeling relaxed after my holiday, I thought nothing of it until my friend, Shaz, noticed the big beam across our living room was cracked. As the beam stabilizes the outside wall, it's a worrying situation, and I'm grateful it doesn't appear to have got any worse since then.

Earthquakes by Phil Stuart

Fast asleep …
Rude awakening-
Chimneys crashing
China breaking.

Rapid heartbeat, foundations shifted.
The earth beneath upheaved and rifted.
Proud peaks are toppled and walls defaced.
Houses cracked with brickwork braced.

Is it random, When's the next?
Will we be maimed? Will we be dressed?
Are we mere specs of complex dust?
That matter not and have no trust?

In Mother Nature who rolls the die,
And places earthquakes where we lie.
Or is the hand of God in the equation-
provoking change within our nation?

Musing aside we know for sure,
Tis not bricks and mortar that matter more.
Than friends and family - neighbours too,
Now counted precious in ways anew.

Day Six by Margaret Simpson

If an earthquake had to happen, its timing could not
have been better. 4.35am last Saturday meant that with
bars closing at 4am, the central city was pretty well empty

and most people tucked up in bed. It was rather scary in the dark but we managed to find our torches after the initial three tremors, which occurred immediately after each other. I hung onto the door frame and Robert stayed in bed. It seemed to go on forever. My first words were, "Are you alright?" At that stage, we still had electricity but it went off fairly quickly. We just had time enough to see that it was mainly books that had fallen off shelves. The house still seemed to be in one piece, and we just rode out the aftershocks until daylight came. We went back to bed and let it get on with it!

Daylight was a relief and as I looked in the garage for my camp gas stove, my adult sons Ed and Will turned up with theirs and we enjoyed a good cup of tea. Probably the most satisfying event of the day! Both their house and ours seemed to be okay. We heard from the other boys, Matthew (who had experienced the Quake as well, in Timaru) and Stuart, and later on, from other family members and friends.

So there we were - very fortunate with only damage to ornaments and pot plants - no pictures broken. Electricity was back on by the afternoon and water was off for three days. Locally, most damage seemed to be to chimneypots. In this area most houses are wooden and built on piles, so they just swayed in the movement. Other parts of the city have sustained serious damage, especially the older buildings in the CBD and a state of emergency is still in place meaning that the general public has to keep away. Some of the smaller suburbs on the coast and also Kaiapoi, a small town, have received serious damage due to liquefaction of the sandy soil. No deaths have occurred which seems amazing. Yesterday we had a serious aftershock thought to be the 6 we had been warned to expect but it turned out to be a 5.1. Even so it was a very sharp jolt. Aftershocks still continue to happen and a sharp jolt can catch you unawares. I think we have had over 350 since the big quake and it is predicted that they will continue possibly for months. We still might get the 6 predicted! Quite a number of our beautiful church buildings have been badly damaged. The trouble is that as buildings are assessed, they keep having to be reassessed with continuing sharp aftershocks. Some families are really struggling in the worst-hit areas - dream homes having to be demolished, children and adults shell-shocked by the uncertainty of the tremors and wonderful people working long, hard hours to get things back to normal as soon as possible. We count our blessings - in this situation we have been very blessed – with protection and safety. There is a lot of thankfulness to God.

A Holyday Experience by Anne Smith

I have been staying with a dear friend who has two prayer partners who meet with her weekly to pray for New Zealand. They pray earnestly (and I must say, loudly) for a considerable time. I don't know how much is in their own language or how much in their prayer tongues. But I know they are genuine and kindly people. All three ladies are Korean and belong to a Korean Presbyterian church. One of them is an Estate Agent in New Zealand; another has been a talented dancer, training the Korean National dance company, as far as I understand it.

When they met on the last Monday in August 2010, there was a strong feeling of oppression, of darkness and the idea of a bird of prey looking for opportunity to attack.

They prayed about it, of course, and one felt the need to fast and pray for three days about whatever the darkness indicated. She did this from midday Tuesday to midday Friday.

When the news of our earthquake came through they knew at once that that had been the topic of their prayers, and praised God for his goodness.

My friend was the one who fasted, and the only one who had lived in Christchurch. She now lives in Auckland with her husband and they support a daughter at Med School. She tells me that she has prayed for New Zealand ever since she came here. "Jesus always says to me 'Christchurch is a very special city, it has my name. I want my name honoured, I want revival.'"

Who knows what influence their prayers had in the economy of God and the outcome of the earthquake?

Damage to St Giles Church in Papanui By Margaret Simpson

A few days after the earthquake, there was an opportunity to see inside St Giles Presbyterian Church in Papanui. Already some tidying up had been done and pews moved away from the damaged brick wall, but bricks and plaster still lay in heaps on the floor. As I looked at the deep gouges in the back of the pews, it really hit home that the quake event, occurring at night, was itself a miracle. The 'what-ifs' of a 7.1 during the day are too terrifying to imagine. Our church is sealed off, although the office is being used. Our first morning service was held in our church lounge. It was communion and folk looked shell-shocked and weary. As stories were shared we distributed the bread and wine, giving thanks to God for keeping us safe. We prayed for the many others in distress and need. Since then we have held each service in the bigger, undamaged hall. Every week we find that we are sitting next to different people - this has been wonderful! In our normal seats we tended to sit in the same place and with the same people. We have met with some new challenges like how to make the drab hall suitable for worship, when it is used all the time for other purposes. Ideas have been discussed and creativity has made the difference. The earthquake has shaken us up. We have had to think outside of the square, but it has brought us together in a new way.

Alan Maxwell shared his thoughts on photographing the damage in St Giles Church.

As the Minister at St Giles since 1981, Reverend John Hunt has had a very long association with the church.

When this photo was taken (carefully), on 10 October 2010, it was more than a month after the initial earthquake, and we had learned that the damage was serious enough that John would not be able to conduct any more services in the church before his retirement on 6 March 2011. So I knew that the damage impacted John in a very personal way, and some of that comes through in this photo. John appears alone, because he had been asked by the SPANZ magazine people for a photograph showing himself and the St Giles church earthquake damage. For me it is important what the photo doesn't show, like the support that the St Giles people have always given each other, and what they continue to do.

Chapter Five – Children and Teenagers React to the Earthquake

Adults were left traumatised and shocked by the events of the 4th September and so were many children. The following accounts tell of reactions by those as young as three as well as some in their teens. Woven into their fear and shock are moments of humour and resilience. For some, writing about their experience has been part of their healing.

Earthquake by Emma-Jane McLennan

A deep rumbling woke me up, violently shaking my bed. What was going on? Suddenly I heard someone yell, "Earthquake!" and I sprang out of bed to brace myself under the doorway, everything shaking and rattling around me. I have never got out of bed that fast on a Saturday morning! But this was a little different than normal. "E-J, get under the table!" Mum called. But I had something to do first … like the rescue workers on TV. I bravely turned back into my room, determined to save … my potted cyclamen. I've never been extremely bright at 4am. Nothing at Science Alive or Te papa ever prepared me for such a big earthquake. Finally, we were all under the table, my family was safe, and we prayed. Once the initial earthquake stopped, the texts started rolling in 'Are you okay?' and different stories of how big it was, what to do, who still had power and water.

Then Mum got up to turn the radio on, and next thing I heard a thump. She had fainted, slumping on the kitchen tiles with her eyes wide open like a zombie, looking through us. Confused, scared I called 111 for the first time in my life but the line was overloaded.

Eventually we got her back underneath the table and sat there through the aftershocks.

Dad went into survival mode, boiling water, found the torches and took down anything breakable. When the sun finally came up, we had a look outside. The water feature statue, which took two people to carry in, had fallen over. The pets were okay, so we went for a walk down the street to check on the neighbours. I have never seen people so friendly. Everyone was amazed simply to be alive, almost excited to see little bubbling volcanoes of silt and water on their lawns. "Wow, look at that," we said, "a crack in the pavement!" We had survived a 7.1, nobody was hurt; it was an amazing, euphoric kind of feeling. We were on the news! It was going to take a while to clean up, so we helped with the silt-digging around town. Every now and then I would wake up at night, my bed shaking again; just a gentle shudder so I wouldn't forget.

My Earthquake Experience by April McLennan, age 13

Shake, shake. Slosh, slosh. Ting, ting, ting! I woke up to these sounds. My room was dark, but I could hear everything shaking, the water sloshing out of the aquarium, and the crystals on my lamp making a 'ting' noise as they smashed into each other. As soon as I was properly conscious, my only thought was 'I need to get up,' even though I don't think I had realised it was an earthquake. Terrified, I felt glued to the bed, unable to get up. That's when my Dad (probably only a couple of seconds later) made it to my two little sisters and my bedrooms, hurrying us under the dining table. Huddling helplessly under the table, waiting for the shaking to stop, my family and I were confused, scared and bewildered. Not long after, the power went out so my Dad had to go searching for torches and candles on that pitch-black September morning. But that wasn't all. My Mum went into the kitchen to turn the radio on, but it didn't have back-up batteries, and of course the power was out. Suddenly, Mum was on the ground, a faraway look in her eyes, and not responding to us. Already being terrified, this just made it worse and to me the whole ordeal felt like a horrible nightmare. My older sister called 111 but of course so many people were calling each other and 111 that the call failed to connect. Eventually, Mum got better and we all sat or lay down under the table, E-J and I texting friends and family to check they were okay.

After what felt like a long time, the sun came up and we had some visitors at our door—friends from around the road. We talked, and then took a walk around our neighbourhood, seeing people, cracks in the pavement and road and little volcanoes of silt that had popped up here and there. I have to admit that when the sun came up everything seemed better, and even as I texted a friend, we wondered whether hockey would still be on. I guess we weren't familiar with what the aftermath could be like and also that the main hockey facility in Christchurch was totalled. That day was strange since there wasn't much we could do to help except keep in touch with people. We ended up with a sunny, beautiful day at home. I am so thankful no one died in that earthquake, I think all us Cantabrians felt extremely proud that we were so strong.

Blog Post by Sanya age 11, September 10th, 2010

Friday night we came home from a conference. And when I went to bed, I felt strange, sort of like I knew something was going to happen but I did not know what.

I was rudely woken up at about 4:35am when my Dad yelled at the top of his voice for us to get out of bed. The house was swaying, shaking, rocking, and creaking. (I sleep in a bunk bed with my little sister) I felt the bunk swaying, shaking, and rocking violently. My first thought was, 'this has to be an earthquake. It could not be anything else.' Anyway, I leapt out of bed, dragging a blanket with me and ran shivering under the nearest door frame. It was the worst shock I've had in my life, because I have never experienced an earthquake or fire before. After getting torches (as there was no power), we ran into the dining room and huddled under the big dining room table (all 10 of us).

By that time, the earthquake had finished and we were feeling aftershocks. It was a big shock for all of us and we did not sleep in, in fact, we got out from under the table at 7:15am. We milked the goats as usual and only twice did we crouch under that table, because of two violent aftershocks, just as I was preparing lunch. They hit, and we leapt under cover and held on.

We have now recovered from the earthquake as we suffered no major damage except for cracks and holes in our concrete slab under the carpet. We do not live far from the epicentre - I think about 17 kilometres. We did not suffer much damage because our house is a modern home and it has a timber frame and bricks over that. We did not get power until Monday afternoon. Yet scientists say we

64

will be expecting an earthquake so big it will crush houses. That would be the Alpine fault line, which will probably hit all of New Zealand. Woe to old houses.

The Wisdom of Children by Kim Allan

Our wee five-year-old reacted with great interest to being moved out of bed at speed. Our house was rocking so hard I fell over twice carrying her out of her bedroom. As Emily stood in the doorway, she and Samuel (aged three) were checking if this was the sort of thing Suzy Cato had told them about on 'Suzy's World.'They then explained to us that we shouldn't worry; it was just the earth's plates moving together and we would be fine. They have both been very sensible about the whole affair!

Nightmare by Katherine Zbijowski, age 13

My eyes instantly flashed open, my mind in a state of sheer panic. Was this real? Was this all a horrible dream? I had no idea at all of what to think. Luckily the rest of my family understood. The rocking of the house gave me the feeling of uncertainty and all I wanted to do was collapse to the ground in tears. Somehow I stayed calm, maybe the shock was too much for me to react to, or maybe deep inside I still thought of it as a dream or at least I hoped it was ... I was living a nightmare that I couldn't wake up from. I only faintly heard my mum yelling my name along with my brother, Theo's. My mind was clouded with frightening questions, and over and over I asked myself, am I going to die?

After what seemed like hours the rumbling of the earthquake subsided. The noise of the earthquake rang in my ears, I still recall the deafening noise, which is best described as a truck ramming through the house. The rumbling and tumbling left me scared stiff, and yet I carried on.

One by one, the aftershocks hit each one worse than the next. It was only when I took a proper look at my surroundings that I noticed the unbroken vase on the floor, with all its contents lying nearby. There I was, sitting in the small, dark, but safe space under the dining room table. There with me sat my family (Mum, Dad and brother Theo). We were all very cramped but no one dared to leave this safe, comforting area. Everyone was becoming more and more nervous from the realisation, that yes, we did just have a major earthquake and all electricity was lost. The rest of my family listened to the radio whereas I stayed in my corner of the enclosed space, waiting in despair for the aftershocks to come. I tried to shut off some of the noise and mask my true feelings. I tried to be brave when I felt the complete opposite. I knew there was more to come, more damage to be made and more frightening moments lying in wait ready to pounce any second.

Dante's Quake Monster by Lois Morgan

I live in Nelson but have grandchildren in Christchurch who were profoundly affected by the quake. Three-year-old Dante was totally convinced that a monster had targeted their house only, and if they could get just get round to Grandma's, a few blocks away, they would be alright! I put together this poem for him in an attempt to put the experience in a more reassuring light.

Dante's Quake Monster

When Earthquake Monster hit the town
A LOT of things came tumbling down
And people sleeping in the night
Woke up with a TREMENDOUS fright!

A rumbling noise was rolling through,
The lights snapped out before they knew,
Out in the streets some giant cracks
Went ziggy zagging through like tracks.

In Dante's house a mighty BOOF!
Sent chimney bricks right through the roof,
The TV did the Highland Fling
And danced around like anything

The kitchen fridge spun on the floor
And tossed the veges out its door,
Oscar and Hugo – they're the cats –
Shot through the catflap fast as rats
But where they went nobody knew –
They stayed away 'till half past two.

Dante and Myah quickly sped
To Mum and Dad's big cuddly bed
Then up jumped Whisky – quite a crowd
Though usually this was not allowed.

Dante was *sure* a Monster's work
Had caused their house to shake and jerk
He thought that they should hurry round
To Grandma's place, on firmer ground
But when they tried to use the phone
It was as dead as Whisky's bone.

The family snuggled up until
The sunlight touched the window sill
And though the house still had the shakes
From other little wiggly quakes
When everything was said and done,
It was SO good to feel the sun.

Chapter Six – Earthquakes and Post Traumatic Stress Disorder

There are four elements to a trauma. It is overwhelming, potentially life threatening, unexpected and it causes fear, horror and helplessness. The person caught up in such an event may feel out of control. It is a known fact that natural disasters can trigger extremely high stress levels that can result in post traumatic stress disorder (PTSD). These events include hurricanes, tornadoes, tsunamis, fires, floods ... and of course, earthquakes. In some ways earthquakes can be more devastating as there is absolutely no warning and no way to predict when one is about to strike. With other events, there is often a period where people can prepare for the disaster and leave the area if necessary. During an earthquake, the ground changes instantly from something stable and secure to something that can't be trusted: a monster that can rear its head at any time and cause immense damage, injury and death. Aftershocks can exacerbate PTSD as they bring repeated trauma – and the aftermath of an earthquake has the potential for further stress.

An acute form of PTSD is generally seen in the first three months after such an event and may be followed by a longer-lasting chronic form. The three core symptoms of PTSD can be loosely grouped as follows:

- Recurring intrusive thoughts accompanied by strong emotions. These include nightmares and flashbacks that make you feel like you're reliving the traumatic event. They can be triggered by a sight, sound or smell associated with earthquakes and may also cause physical symptoms like an accelerated heart rate.

- Numbness, avoidance and detachment. Strong negative emotions from an event like an earthquake may grow stronger instead of fading with time. You avoid the scene of the trauma or places that remind you of it. Parts of the trauma may be blocked out of your memory. Movies and news reports on a similar theme are avoided. Emotional numbness is common as is a loss of interest in life and usual activities.
- Hyperarousal is described as the nervous system being on red alert. You overreact to loud noises, feel angry and may have difficulty relaxing or sleeping. Panic symptoms such as palpitations and sweaty palms are triggered by excess adrenaline in your system.

Many people in Christchurch were traumatised after the September earthquake and some had not recovered when the February shake struck. Liz, who lived in Christchurch at the time of the September earthquake shared her story in the hopes of helping others and bringing insight and understanding into how PTSD can affect a person.

PTSD and the Christchurch Earthquake by Liz

I don't think my feelings or thoughts during the earthquake were anything different from anyone else in the city. I definitely wish I had never experienced it. When the shaking woke me, for a couple of seconds I tried to work out what was going on. I initially thought 'this is what an epileptic fit feels like,' and that I was trapped in a convulsion, the shaking of which had awoken me. I was not used to the feeling and the increasing size and frequency of movement. An earthquake was definitely not on my radar, especially in Christchurch. However, I quickly worked out what was going on and threw myself into the landing so I was near an internal wall. I had immediate maternal-like concern for my housemates who were foreigners, but luckily only one was at home that night - a French girl. I was concerned that she would not know what to do and shouted to her to join me. It was pitch black but I knew the lights would not work, and we could only find each other by voices. She fell down next to me and we cuddled together leaning next to the internal wall. I remember feeling the need to reassure her, saying it would finish soon, and provided information like the power would be out, and that there would be aftershocks straight after, etc.

However, while I was trying to provide this source of reason and comfort, and thinking of the right things to say, my mind was going in an opposite direction thinking such negative thoughts. 'What if this turns out to be the biggest earthquake ever?' or 'what if the house disappears in to the earth,' and 'what if this is not in Christchurch and is in Auckland, how bad is it there?' Although I was convincing myself it would stop within a minute or two, there was a thought in my mind of 'what if this is the one, the one that never stops?' I had to try and talk my mind down and say to cross that bridge when I come to it, and to try and keep as calm as possible. The shaking stopped. We stayed where we were for an hour after that. I kept trying to crawl back into my room in the dark to find my torch,

71

location of which I thought I knew for emergencies, but same as my radio it took me some time to find it. What interested me was that on the landing it was reasonably stable, but in my bedroom, the movement was still hugely noticeable. Two seconds in there, and I felt the need to go straight back to the landing.

After an hour, although it was still dark, and we still felt the slightest movement and rolling, things had calmed down to the point where we felt we could go for a look outside. Upon going downstairs, I think it really hit me that there had been an earthquake. My mountain bike had been thrown from one side of the hall to the other, there was a broken vase in the front room, some food items on top of the microwave had fallen off, but no cupboards had opened. Everything was surreal, and as we were going out of the front door, we realised that all the other neighbours were coming out of their properties at exactly the same time. We all went out on the street for a look. Everything was pitch black, and you could see police cars running around, along with the odd speeding boy racer who must have figured the police were preoccupied with other things. We then went back into the house. My housemate tried to get some sleep but with the aftershocks that wasn't for long. I went in to a therapeutic cleaning frenzy. During times of stress, I clean - like I absolutely blitzed my room. Then with us both awake we decided to go for a walk through the city to see what was happening.

Upon reflection, walking around after an earthquake was a stupid idea, but I was rostered to work at 8am, and going back to bed was pointless. I also wanted to show for my shift as although I knew I would not be working, part of me felt if I did show then maybe the earthquake was not that bad.

As soon as we set off and crossed the Avon by the Bridge of Remembrance the damage became clear although nothing was looked to be completely collapsed. All the shelves had fallen over in the mini supermarket on the corner, and they had a sign on the door saying 'no looters.' A few doors along in a clothing shop's window display, mannequins were lying on their sides looking eerie due to the fact they had no arms. I was quick to point out the earthquake-proof structure of one of the banks. However, when we got closer, we realised that all the glass had fallen out of its tall structure and was lying intact in crumbled sheets on the floor. Around the city damage was evident, but I realised that the damage was in pockets, like one block was fine and the next one was not. And, of course, as soon as I got to work I was sent away, but I was not alone in turning up.

We walked from there down to the supermarkets, in case there was post-earthquake panic buying, but everything looked fine, so stupidly we said we would come back later. We should have got water and bread at that time, as they sold out later on. I went for a walk by myself back towards the CBD, as I had an urge to feed my Starbucks and coffee addiction. Understandably, everywhere was shut so it could be checked and cleaned up, and it was not on my radar that the water would be undrinkable in the coffee shops, hence affecting their business.

As I walked around the city centre I was shouted at by an English guy. I went to see what he was looking at and he was frantically pointing at a building with columns that seemed about to collapse. Inside was a family refusing to leave, and although we were signalling to them to come out of the building they just waved back. Pedestrians, albeit a lot of rubberneckers, were walking under the building without a care in the world. We grabbed gates from nearby road-works on the tram tracks to seal the street. I then said I would go tell the police so they could help get the family out of the building. I should point out at this point that there was no cordon as such, and only one or two streets in the city centre were closed. This was about five hours after the initial quake. I remember at the time thinking this was odd with all the high-rise buildings around, and broken glass windows, but had faith in the Civil Defence plans of the country and thought it must be okay, although it blatantly was not. The officer I went to tell about the building about to collapse told me to stop talking and go away, but I stood my ground. "No! Listen to me! People are going to be hurt." He listened then, and let me through the cordoned-off street to talk to his supervisor. The police got the family out of the building pretty quickly.

I returned home. One of the plus points of living between the hospital and the police headquarters was that we got the power back on pretty quickly. I made a pot of coffee. I don't know why but the smell of coffee meant so much that morning and stood out more - maybe I had heightened senses after the shake. There was a constant rumbling noise, and occasional roll, but we both questioned whether that was the ongoing earthquake, or if it was just us still shaking! The only time this was really confirmed was when there was an aftershock of a decent size, and these happened frequently through the day. Adrenaline was probably pumping through the pair of us at that point, but we were handling it pretty well and laughing it off. As the day progressed, we made the decision we would sleep in the front room, so we were both together, and had tables nearby to hide under, and were nearer the door should we need to get out in a rush.

For the following days we had our little camp in the lounge, and followed the Civil Defence instructions of staying in as much as we could. We were pretty addicted to Geonet, and the internet and news, whilst trying to keep informed of any urgent information we might need. Noticeable aftershocks almost became like a game of bingo, with, 'I think that was just over a 4,' guesses going on.

The day after the earthquake was the most beautiful warm day, with the most perfect sunshine. I insisted in cooking breakfast, unusual for me as cooking is neither a love of mine or a forte. We were both inspired at times

75

separate to each other to go for a run and try and have some kind of exercise, and later found ourselves walking around the city on a bit of an earthquake sightseeing tour. We even went back to the park as I had found lots of cracks and lines from the quake, and it seemed a good opportunity to get photos for Facebook and future grandchildren.

Mid walk we ducked back home for an extra layer as the temperature was dropping. As soon as we passed through the door, there was a massive aftershock, which instantly made us want to get back out in to the glorious sunshine. It also reminded us that we were still in danger. For the rest of the walk we were more subdued, and less in love with the day we were experiencing. We knew as we returned home that darkness would fall, and it would be another difficult and testing night of trying to get sleep between aftershocks and constant movements, with the uncertainty of another big one hitting and if something could possibly happen to hurt us during the night. One night's sleep would be relatively unbroken, followed by another one with no sleep at all, where we constantly threw ourselves under furniture to try and protect ourselves. This almost became a reflex movement after some time. By day three and four I was really questioning the amount of aftershocks that were taking place, and was texting friends to see if it was normal. Something felt really wrong to me as you expect a few aftershocks but not that many.

I lasted in Christchurch until day six I think. The morning of day five we were both rudely awaken by a 5.1 aftershock, which to me had the velocity of being more violent than the original shake. It could only be described as someone picking up the house and banging it on the table three times really hard. We were out of there. Then when we went outside one of the neighbours pointed out our chimneys had popped and were a crumbled mess on top of the roof. My house mate had a nose bleed with every aftershock that morning, which was unusual for her. I found two Scottish backpackers in shock up the street crying, and we went up to a friend of my housemate in Addington, when the boiler started leaking. Others met us there and we piled up to Riccarton to find somewhere to have a coffee as we all felt the need to get out of the house. Unfortunately McDonalds was all that was open (McDonalds is always open. It was even open three hours after the original quake), but coffee was not on the menu due to no tap water. The people I sat with were all in shock. One girl had been absolutely terrorised by her work colleagues about all the things that could happen such as a bigger shake and a volcano. They pretty much told her she was going to die whilst laughing and joking about it – not caring that she did not need to hear that at that time. I tried to encourage everyone to have a break out of town as I had friends in Timaru. They seemed reluctant to go but everyone definitely needed the mental break.

I decided I had mentally had enough. With every aftershock more and more cracks appeared in the ceiling, including a supporting beam and the external foundations. Our landlord said there was nothing wrong with the property and refused to get a proper building inspector in as he said there was nothing to inspect. But I had had enough.

Unfortunately, I had experienced a lot of other stress prior to the earthquake and was surprised that I had been coping as I really had little left, and I was at the point where physically I could not handle one more aftershock. I just didn't want to experience anymore. I arranged to go to Timaru the next day to stay with friends for a few nights and also to collect my van which I had down there. I wanted my van so I could shift stuff quickly and also to provide transport to move and sleep in if needed.

That night we stayed on the floor at someone's house in another part of Addington. This area stunk of sulphur, which was scary as we wondered if we were on top of a volcano. We also discussed the noise as aftershocks were much quieter in this house and not as noisy as we had experienced in town. We thought maybe the structure of the earth under our house was different because the house was next to the banks of the Avon - but we were just guessing. The quieter house made a big difference to our sleep that night.

The next morning, I left early on the bus. The others left too, heading up to Picton. I was so grateful to be away from Christchurch and to see my van. I think I had coped pretty well with my flight and fight response post the quake, but upon removing myself from the city strange things started happening to me. I seemed to go into delayed shock. Twenty-four hours after I had been in Timaru my friends were having a dinner party where I was staying, but I could not handle being round loads of people, or indoors. I kept going outside to sit on the step as I just wanted air and quiet and could not handle the noise, especially from the kids playing. I could not speak at times, and was crying for no reason. If I was indoors in any room, I could picture the house falling on me. It was as if my subconscious had taken over. Indoors I would be sitting there watching TV or talking and out of the corner of my eye I could see the room shaking, even though it was not.

Sleep was impossible; as soon as my head hit the pillow I was wide awake. Once I was asleep, I would wake every hour ready to throw myself under a table. I could not handle going to the supermarket as I felt the high shelves were going to fall on me, and also could not handle walking through open spaces such as paddocks, or crossing the road. My body felt horrible. My muscles in my neck and upper back became that locked that I ended up having to see a chiropractor with a nerve trapped in my shoulder. I was desperate to return to normality but my sleep patterns grew worse the more tired and distressed I got. I sought medication from my doctor but unfortunately he misdiagnosed me and gave me medicine for depression, missing the shock I was in. After a couple of weeks I took myself off these meds which were such a high dose that I had full-on withdrawal symptoms, adding vomiting, sweating and chills to my list of ailments.

Things are now a lot better for me, but I still have PTSD symptoms. I still see a chiropractor and the corner of the room will start shaking for no reason whatsoever. Noises still make me jump, especially loud cars shaking the house like trucks, but sleep has pretty much returned to normal. I am currently choosing to do a course of study, rather than working, as I do not feel fully up to it just yet, and feel I would not give my professionalism justice while I am still occasionally hallucinating earthquakes. And I cook. Since the quake I have been into cooking and baking, something I had no patience for before. This may sound like some weird coping strategy, but I find something amazingly calming and centering in this new interest. I almost feel like it is an achievement being able to stay in the kitchen for long enough to be able to do something without any shakes, and feel lucky to be able to do so.

I think people's naivety is the biggest thing that tested me and upset me in light of the quake. People have made me to be a drama queen when I say I wish I had never been in it, and they play it down like, it's just an earthquake, they happen in New Zealand, like they are a everyday occurrence and I am exaggerating, but it is something I would never choose to experience again. I have a feeling associated with the ground shaking, which is like a smell, which I guess comes from the many thoughts that come from a quake, but is to me like a sense, and I hope never to experience another quake. I know before I was in it I always thought yeah the ground would shake around then I would be fine as long as I am not injured. I have always been a reasonably strong (if that is the right word) person, who, through my interest in outdoor sports and outdoor education, has trained in lots of rescue work and techniques, and through that the subject of shock and trauma has much been discussed. But in this my mind and subconscious just took over. I was surprised at quite how much, and how it was so out of my hands and I could not control it.

I do not understand the looters. I do not understand the psychology of someone whose first thought straight after an earthquake would be that of stealing. I think for the majority, shock, safety, and family was the immediate thought, not going out to steal. Plus shopping. The morning of the big aftershock when we went to Riccarton there were immediate queues outside the mall. Even though it was closed, they were keen for it to reopen. I am always up for a bargain and the chance to eye up the latest fashions, but again, it was the last thought in my mind to go be stuck in the mall at that time.

I was surprised when I initially listened to the radio on the morning of the quake as there appeared to be little in the way of Civil Defence announcements, just reports that an earthquake had happened in Christchurch. Again, as mentioned before, I expected to hear instructions, like I suppose I expected the city centre to be closed if it was dangerous, but it seemed like people were in shock, and were having delayed reactions to the fact that an earthquake had actually taken place. I was definitely disappointed in my landlord who seemed more interested in retaining tenants, then safety, as he expressed some of them had already left some of his thirty properties around town.

I unfortunately got my fingers burnt by how bad people's naivety and ignorance can get. I lost my job in Christchurch too and I went back to collect my belongings, friends convinced me to stay with them for a while until I was stronger. Everything felt unreal and I knew that it was time for me to stop and look after myself; to nurse myself back to health and have some time out to recharge the batteries. This as I have previously mentioned was not just to do with the earthquake. However the earthquake was the final straw that broke the camel's back, and was initially haunting me as I had no reserves left to be able to process what I had been through.

One of the first comments made to me by a friend in Timaru was that my feelings were only based on what I had seen on TV, not how I was really reacting. I have never watched a programme where I woke up every hour when I am trying to sleep, or have agoraphobic type symptoms. This made me upset, but I let it go as I knew that it was just someone else's opinion. I was only fully reassured when I heard of a group of children at a farm stay in Timaru who were experiencing the same symptoms as me four to six weeks after the quake; who were waking up every hour screaming, although they seemed to have the capacity to almost laugh the quake off during the day time. The meds I was prescribed made me pretty zombified which I did not want. All I wanted was to sleep.

I also found it hard to get over the earthquake, much as I wanted to, which I expressed to those nearest to me. At this time, my friendships in this town came to an end. Instead of support, I was told I was neurotic, pathetic, obsessive, negative, and stupid for proactively wanting to get counselling at that time, and that I had a need to surround myself with these agencies and get rescued. Here is a snippet of what one of them put on my Facebook at that time: 'Hmmmm so what is the name for someone who is clingy, unable to take responsibility for themselves, constantly in need of reassurance, neurotic, avoids confronting issues, sensationalises minor events and makes them into a HUGE issue when really there isn't one.'

One particular person took it upon themselves to try and make me jump, banging hard on my car if I was in it, or on my bedroom door, as they saw humour, and empowerment in this. I thought I had gone somewhere for a good break upon the suggestion of my friends. However, this turned to work against me and initially made me worse. Needless to say this was pretty difficult, but somehow I removed myself from this negative circle pretty quickly and started afresh in Nelson. I was lucky to not feel alone during this time as I had regular contact with friends in Nelson where I previously lived, which kept me going. I know my symptoms would have got worse if I had remained in that negative and unsupportive environment and I needed to be around supportive people at that time.

Upon reflection, I think the biggest thing that affected me from the quake was the volume and frequency of aftershocks. I think if it had just been the initial quake alone, I would probably have been fine. But being on constant guard, really threw me. Through commitments I have, I've had to visit Christchurch a couple of times since September. Both times have been very testing and have made me quite nauseous, but I have been blessed that the aftershocks seemed to stop when I was in town.

Hearing of the newest earthquake in Christchurch made me feel instantaneously ill. I was in the bottom floor of the new hospitality block in Nelson Polytechnic and was just returning back from lunch to start again at 1pm. As I

83

walked through the door I heard about it as one of my class was on his cell phone to his friend in Christchurch where the person had said it was worse than September and quickly hung up. We knew things were bad as we were trying to call each other's phones and the networks were affected. When I got home and saw the TV at 3pm, I burst into tears, and was almost sick. Luckily I had a pre-arranged appointment with my counsellor that afternoon which helped somewhat, but for the rest of the day, I was a bit shocked. I thought my PTSD symptoms would become far worse again. However I seem to have been reasonably alright, bar some very strong dreams. Two nights after the new quake, I woke up wondering what had happened to the people that were swimming at the time in the Centennial Pool, somewhere I used to go regularly in Christchurch. Every room I go in I wonder what it would be like to be trapped in, but this seems to be passing again. My immediate circle of friends at the moment are supportive, however do not truly understand. I wanted to make emergency bags and water bottles up to help us if there were problems here, which they saw as me being a little over reactive, but were happy for me to do. This I suppose is down to the good old Kiwi attitude of 'she'll be right', rather than proactivity. My family in the UK definitely did not understand. After I had told my dad of the initial earthquake in September, he asked me what the weather was doing One of my class in Nelson returned to Christchurch to help family affected by the quake and had his car stolen when he got there - again more incredible stories of stupidity at that time.

I have been saying since the earthquake in September that the amount of aftershocks and the fact that scientists have been saying for years that a big one over 8 is due on the Alpine Pacific Fault that runs through Nelson and Wellington, that this could be a build up to a big one letting off steam in Christchurch to try and stop it from happening. My friends and I looked back on the history of quakes on the Geonet website, and could not find anything with this many aftershocks post a quake in the history of New Zealand. Therefore I am scared to feel it again.

Chapter Seven –Visitors to Christchurch and Locals who Missed the Big Shake

After the September earthquake, attention was focused mostly on people who lived in Christchurch. However, there were other groups of people who were also deeply impacted. These included folk who were visiting Christchurch at the time, locals who were out of town, and family and friends of people who lived in Christchurch. The effect on them was also one of great emotion, shock and disbelief.

A Horrendous Experience by Lois and Lindsay Penno of Napier

We went to bed in the Copthorne Hotel, Durham Street, Christchurch, on the eighth floor. I woke at 4:12am, and as we were flying back to Napier at 7:00am we had decided to have a cup of tea and then shower We packed our suitcase the night before, thank goodness. The quake occurred at 4:35am and the noise preceding it was horrendous. Then it hit! It is just so hard to describe the absolute terror as the hotel was violently weaving backwards and forwards and making the most horrible concrete screeching noises - and it was so loud. Lindsay thinks that we were going at least a metre backwards and forwards and it was incredibly terrorising. And it went on and on and on. We thought we were going to die!

Eventually it stopped and we got up and got dressed in the dark – absolutely no lighting - and I even managed to find my jewellery and handbag. At this point a female staff member came around banging on the doors and screaming to evacuate and you could just hear the panic and fear in her voice. When I got out of bed my legs were shaking with fright. We had to go down eight flights of stairs on the outside of the building which was all floor to ceiling windows and with water pouring down the stairs our journey was really, really terrifying. During the long walk down the stairs, our daughter, Dee, rang us to see if we were still alive.

It was freezing cold outside and we huddled in the middle of the street. Some people were only in their PJ's with no shoes and had a blanket around them. There was a Japanese couple with a little girl about a year old and they were trying to keep her warm. We stayed outside for an hour and then they got us to go back inside to the foyer and restaurant and they eventually found some candles. When lit, we discovered horrendous cracks in the beams and wires hanging down everywhere. In hindsight, we should never have gone back into the building.

At about 7:30am they took us around by foot to their other hotel, The Millenium, which had suffered very little damage. We sat in the foyer and restaurant and it looked like a war zone with people in all stages of undress. Eventually they put on muesli and fruit for us. At this point Lindsay became very cold and shivered uncontrollably but I think it was just fright. At about 10:30am we all walked back to our hotel and a member of the staff came up with us to our room on the eighth floor (puffing when we got there) whilst we got our belongings and went to the loo as there was no flushing at the other hotel and you can imagine the state of the loos with all those people.

The whole experience was surreal with buildings falling down and in various stages of decline. There were Police on every corner in the CBD and they were excellent.

When we got back to the Millenium Hotel there was a man playing on the beautiful grand piano and Lindsay said that it was the Titanic experience as apparently the band played on while the ship was sinking. All this time, of course, we had massive aftershocks.

Our daughter, Dee and her partner, Alan, were staying in the Ibis Hotel but the staff did not come around and tell them to evacuate and when they got out into the street, the two staff members on the desk were in the middle of the road. They came around and saw us and then went back to their hotel where they were told the city was being evacuated and they would have to leave. Incidentally, many people would have seen the fire in the city and that was very close to their hotel.

We were offered a very nice room on the second floor of the Hotel Millenium for the night but they did not have water and how would they have coped with a fire, so we decided to evacuate. Lindsay went and got our car from the basement of our hotel but could not bring it into the CBD so the four of us hot footed it to the car and went out to a Christchurch suburb called Merivale where we got motel rooms. We just wanted to leave the CBD – it was so frightening with tremors happening all the time.

When we walked down to the shops for breakfast that morning, so many of the shops were condemned and just the previous morning we had walked around the same area. It was completely devastated and we all could have been killed. We were stunned at the devastation in Merivale but we went out there because we did not want to be in a multi-storey building above ground level.

We had to wait until 3:00pm the next day to get a flight back to Napier and home has never looked so good. We have since found out that there were major cracks in the structure of our hotel and we never should have gone back inside. Incidentally, the hotel did not have either candles or torches and had to go to another of their hotels to get them. Having said that, the staff were very solicitous. We were both shattered emotionally after our experience and hope never to witness an earthquake of this magnitude again. Also, the slightest sound and we both froze. I think it will take a very long time for us to get over our ordeal and we were both so traumatised. I repeat, we both thought we were going to die. In fact, it took ten days for us to be able to sleep again.

As a footnote to the above, a few years ago my husband built a sea-going yacht and he and I sailed it to Australia. For the two weeks it took us, we never saw the sun and the moon such were the storm conditions. However, in hindsight the 40 second earthquake in Christchurch was far worse.

A Story with a Difference by Janette Busch of Christchurch

My story might be a bit different. I was in Hobart, Australia, at a conference when the earthquake hit. I got woken by a call on my cell phone at three in the morning (time difference) from my daughter in Christchurch.

She had been trying to contact me since the earthquake struck but I'd turned my phone off at the first chirp, thinking it was a text from someone who didn't know I was in Australia; in the darkness I had no idea what the time was. I'd already woken my roommate two hours earlier the previous day when I'd forgotten to change my phone to Australian time. After about twenty minutes something made me put the phone under the pillow to muffle the sound as best I could and turn it on again; that's when I got the call.

"I just thought you'd like to know before you heard it from someone else that we've had a big earthquake in Christchurch," Catherine said.

I checked that she and her husband were not harmed. It turned out she'd spent quite some time trying to wake him and then persuading him it was an earthquake worth responding to.

"It was the glassware breaking in the kitchen that convinced us both to get out of bed," she said.

I asked if she had been in touch with her brother. She had, and Andrew was fine – he had ridden out the earthquake in bed.

I spent the rest of the time until daylight huddling in the toilet (trying to muffle the sound of my voice – unsuccessfully, I expect) while getting updates from them.

You might be thinking it was easier for me than for those of you who in Christchurch; I can assure you it was not - the emotional roller coaster and deepening anguish I felt as I tried to find out what was happening in Christchurch, while being surrounded by people who had never experienced an earthquake, who persisted in asking me how my house was rather than how I was; and I wasn't doing very well. Early reports, however, were that my house was fine.

By mid afternoon it all got too much for me and I phoned my daughter and sobbed down the phone my distress at not being there. "It's my people, it's my city, it's my country - I want to be there to help," I cried (tears are streaming down my face now as I write these words). It was the not knowing that I found so difficult. By this time I had been on the internet and seen the devastation in the central city.

Calmly Catherine replied, "What do you want to know?"

She and her husband are volunteer ambulance officers with St John and had been mobilised soon after the earthquake and spent the day checking on people. It was only then that I understood that my city had not been completely destroyed - the Westende Jewellery image was the only one shown by the media at that time. My city would survive.

I flew home as planned the next day. As I waited in the departure lounge with others at Melbourne Airport it was very obvious who was going to Christchurch. We were the ones sitting quietly and not talking – thinking our own thoughts. None of us knew what we were returning to.

That was the night of the extremely high north-west winds in Canterbury and we hit them as the plane tried to cross the Southern Alps. I was touched when all my family met the plane despite the late hour.

Coming back, I was thrown into what everybody else was experiencing and was very fearful and jumpy for the first week (my bed seemed to be the safest place to be). I packed myself a survival kit that I kept outside my bedroom door for about six weeks or so. I was able to return to work on the Friday after the earthquake and having something else to do other than cook biscuits for people in shelters and drop in centres, was good.

I thought about the biscuits after a bottle of red wine fell from a shelf on top of a 5 kg bag of sugar. It seemed silly to waste the sugar so I discarded the red stained sugar and used the rest to make the biscuits – lots of them.　　Now, I'm living in a house that has lost a chimney, is developing more cracks and with floors that are not level. It's a time of waiting, of not knowing, of learning to live with uncertainty; and I expect it will remain like this for far longer than any of us expect. Note to self: I must remember to say, "My house has got piles" rather than "I've got piles" when talking about the pile damage to my house.

Not in New Zealand by Ruth Linton of Tauranga

Like many New Zealanders I was stunned when I heard of the Canterbury earthquake. Earthquakes occur in distant places such as China and Haiti, not here in New Zealand! Then came the images of destruction, both of property and people's confidence and livelihood. When the aftershocks continued to pepper the region I suddenly realised people couldn't just go and live safely somewhere else; there weren't enough houses or jobs elsewhere. I was overwhelmed with a sense of sorrow and hopelessness. Many times I wept for the people affected and for the region. The quake had come unexpectedly both in time and in the area affected. No one could have predicted it; there were no warning signs; no one could have been prepared. I became profoundly grateful that where I live, at least for now, we have a chance to prepare for each day. I have the opportunity to live life to the full and to continue to reach out with Christian love to those who continue to suffer uncertainty and hardship. This poem was born out of my feelings about the earthquake.

PREPARED

0600 HOURS…
I look around the sullen beach, inhale the salt-rich
air
Wind slashes the pingao, churns the choppy surface
of the gray-green deep,
And shreds the waves that smash the shells high on
the sand;
See northward low slung clouds haze headlands,
islands out to sea.
The land-ward hills are topped with weighty clouds
that fan
Out shoreward as a giant hand—foretellers of a
pending storm.
Subdued, I hurry home, prepare for rain—grab the
washing off the line-
Perform the outside chores before I'm forced to
stay indoors.

Another day is born…
Translucent azure sky with sheen of sunrise gold;
A delicate sea breeze that blows soft kisses on my
cheek.
The glass-blue sea like jelly slides to meet the sand.
I see a log-ship moored and islands, sharply-
outlined, stand,
The hills defined: alive, aglow with light of rising
sun.
I saunter home; prepare to dry the laundry in fresh
air.
I slap on sunblock and a shady hat and garden:
weed

94

And plant and prune. Then bask and tan in midday
heat.
0435 HOURS...
There is no chance; we can't prepare when
earthquake strikes
And dumps me out of bed amid the freshly-
generated dust
And crumpled displaced crockery. The cracked and
gaping walls
Leer, mocking as I pick my way through desiccated
glass
To quaking freedom on the dew-damp lawn, once
level, now
A mini mountain range beside the crooked
crumbling wall.

I look around...
I'm not prepared for what I see, for such
destructive mess!
We'd looked ahead: built soundly and insured our
home.
How could we be prepared? We had no warning
but
The eerie silence of the birds, and then the
rumbling roar-
Tectonic plates in combat in karate-mode with
shattering results.
Again I look around to greet our neighbours, little-
known,
United as they share their fear and grief. They share
with all

Some practical relief as each is qualified; unnerved
And dazed, but as we speak and serve we show we
care.

And so time passes...
We can look up and find that God's still there. His
throne cannot be swayed.
And though he let the earth be moved, His
compassion was displayed
Ensuring none has perished; so with joy we render
praise.
Our human minds attempt to fathom why He would
allow
The earth to shake; perhaps it was the groans and
tremors of
The earth's travail while with eagerness it waits to
see
The revelation of the sons of the God. It's then it is
released
   From bondage into liberty when God descends
And ushers in His kingdom and eternity.

The Christchurch Earthquake by Hilary Colquhoun of Picton

I live in Picton and I don't always sleep well. The
morning of 'the big earthquake' I was listening to the
national radio, wishing I were asleep. I couldn't believe it
when the announcer said there had been a very big quake
in the Garden City. Oh, it *was* an earth-quake! I had felt it
very slightly.

My sister, Marcia, lived there. She'd be all right –

we were used to them as we had hundreds of them when we were kids in the Manawatu, but they were mostly mild ones. However, I decided to ring straight away – they did say it was a big one. I couldn't believe how frightened she sounded. Little did we know it was the forerunner of many more – and not all little ones.

Then I decided to ring my life-long friend, Dulcie, who, like me, lives alone. She was delighted that I had thought of her. A little later, I rang my step-grandson, who boarded with three other young men in his parents' house. They were fine. They had all rolled over and gone back to sleep again. In fact, the phone ringing didn't even wake up my grandson so I spoke to one of the others. When I finally did speak to him, he hadn't been fazed at all. He was sleeping in his parents' water bed and he just lay back and watched the walls going in and out!

A Rumble and Shake in Timaru by Matthew Simpson

It began with a rumble then a shake! A shake that went on and on and on. It was early hours of the morning when the earthquake hit the seaside town of Timaru. I was with my family in our small home in the middle of town. I have been in an earthquake before so I knew from the sound it was a quake. With vigour I ran up and down the hall yelling for my family to arise. The house at this point was shaking violently, making horrendous groaning sounds as it twisted back and forth. Luckily our house is weatherboard so did not sustain any damage. I know from experience it isn't a good idea to go outside while a quake is still happening but I couldn't help myself. After checking everyone was OK, I popped my head out the front door and, to my surprise, the trees and lights down the street were swaying back and forth like they were lying on a bowl of jelly. What a sight! A sight that still plays on my mind even to this day.

Recollections of Christchurch by Dorothy Ade of South Africa

During 2009 and 2010 I spent three months with my husband in Christchurch and in that time we got to know the city quite well. It's one of the prettiest cities we have ever visited. The layout, the gardens, the buildings, the facilities, the shopping malls cannot be faulted and if it were possible we would, without hesitation, make it our home. We vaguely talked to a friend about earthquakes while we were there and he told us that many of the buildings in Christchurch had been built to withstand earthquakes, but at no time did we ever consider that an earthquake might happen either in Christchurch or elsewhere in New Zealand.

It was with surprise and shock that we heard the news of the earthquake which rocked and rattled Christchurch on 4 September 2010. Our elder daughter sent us a text almost immediately after it happened but we did not read it until about 7am New Zealand time. Naturally we were relieved to hear that our New Zealand family was safe and that there had been no reported deaths, which was a miracle when one considers the death and destruction caused by the Haiti earthquake of the same magnitude. When we woke up on our Saturday morning (we are 11 hours behind New Zealand) we learned that the electricity was reconnected and there were several emails from our daughter with photos covering the damage in the CBD.

It was some weeks before we realized that almost all of Christchurch had been hit in some way or other and while we can be thankful that there was no loss of life, Christchurch as we had seen it, would never be the same again. New buildings will in time replace old buildings which held countless memories for some. We have been kept up to date with news of the clean-up progress and you can be thankful that you have an organized and efficient city council who appear to be coping admirably with the disaster.

We think of all those who have lost their homes and in some cases, businesses as well, and while some of you are downhearted or despondent, just hang in there and look forward to a brighter future in a city where a disaster has drawn the people closer together. The river Avon still runs through the city and the flowers which make the city so attractive in spring will continue to blossom and flourish. Life goes on.

Chapter Eight – The 22nd February 2011

People tend to get comfortable when life follows predictable routines. We get caught up in our small circle of family members and close friends and we focus on our needs and wants. We pass our neighbours with a wave and a smile but hardly take time to connect with them. The people that surround us in malls, on the roads, and at events are a faceless crowd. A major natural disaster such as the Christchurch earthquakes changes all that in a matter of seconds. Instead of being surrounded by comfort, safety and security, people are suddenly homeless, injured, traumatised, cut off from electricity and water and shops and some are left bereaved. The September earthquake was an overwhelming shock to Christchurch but the February earthquake was devastating.

As the shaking started at 12:51pm on the 22nd February 2011, buildings crumbled across the city. Facades fell, foundations shifted and the PGC and CTV buildings collapsed. An almighty dust cloud enveloped the CBD and people screamed in terror as they scrambled to safety. Thousands of cars were trapped in multilevel car parks and other were obliterated by falling masonry. Two buses were crushed, killing a number of passengers. In many streets silt burst through the tarmac, and also infiltrated homes, stores and businesses. Rivers of evil smelling water swirled along roads and silt volcanoes formed as people watched.

Emergency services were mobilised extremely quickly and uninjured members of the public were urged to head home. Those whose cars were accessible drove slowly out of the stricken city while thousands left on foot. The people outside of the CBD were also heading home and within minutes of the earthquake, the city was gridlocked. A journey that normally took 15 minutes by car took over three hours that day. At the same time, the phone networks were completely jammed as people tried desperately to call and text loved ones.

As Christchurch residents struggled homewards, the breaking news was already being aired by radio and television. The live footage of the horror unfolding in the city was a nightmare that none of us could have envisaged – and the images will remain in our hearts and minds forever.

I published the following account on my blog as events unfolded that day.

The First 18 Hours

12 Noon I have a few things to do in Riccarton. I pick up a cheque for Kirstin, post some Trade Me orders and draw some cash. It's Tim's 21st tomorrow but he wants a celebration dinner tonight. My next stop is Northlands Mall where I pull out my shopping list and head to one of the stores that sells cheap novelties.

12:51 I pick up some balloons, a party banner and a badge saying Birthday Boy. *Tim will like that. It'll appeal to his sense of humour.* I'm heading to the till to pay when there's a low rumbling sound and everything starts to shake. Aftershock! The motion increases and people start screaming. I grab onto the shelving unit next to me as the floor heaves beneath my feet. Then a large lighting panel crashes from the ceiling, missing me by inches. It sways in front of me, suspended by a power cable. I look up, step back and try and keep my footing. My heart races wildly as crockery shatters around me and more lighting panels fall. *This is a big one. I thought it was all over.*

12:52 The shaking subsides and people stream from stores, crying, shaking, alarms shrieking all around. I drop my shopping on a shelf and follow. In spite of my shock, my journalistic instincts surface and I snap a few photos as I head to open air. People are orderly as they move towards their cars but a big group clusters around the entrance to the mall. A lady is helped out by work colleagues and sits on a stone under a tree. Another woman lies on the floor in a foetal position, sobbing, face covered. My arms and hands are tingling with pins and needles and feel numb and strange. It must be the shock.

13:02 I try for ten minutes to text the children and call Kevin but the phone lines are jammed. I walk down the ramp to the underground parking to find my car. A dozen alarms echo through the air and I can't wait to get out. Water sprays from overhead pipes and metal conduit is buckled and twisted. I drive up the ramp to find the traffic backed up. As I wait in a queue to leave the mall area, another earthquake hits. I find out later that it's a 5.7. I watch in horrified fascination as the gigantic three storey concrete wall to my right waves and bends like a piece of plastic. It's a wonder of modern architecture that it doesn't shatter.

13:30 The five minute journey home takes 30 minutes and as I sit in queues of cars, I watch silt volcanoes bubbling on roadsides and see a chimney that has fallen halfway through a roof. Back home our house appears undamaged but speakers have fallen, cupboards are open, the contents of my sewing box are strewn across the stairs, and bottles and pictures have fallen. The dogs are subdued and distressed.

14:30 The children are all accounted for and Kevin is safe. I get a text from Chantelle saying her school won't let them out unless they are collected. My son Jason comes and we drive down to Burnside High. As we walk across the field, a 5.5 aftershock hits and the trees, cars and grass undulate. The earth isn't supposed to do this. It's supposed to be dependable and solid. Pupils mill around. Girls are red-eyed and clinging to each other and staff are trying to organise them into divisions. 3000 pupils to account for is no laughing matter. I finally get a text to say Chantelle is at a friend's house opposite the school.

15:30 I watch the non-stop footage on TV and mourn for those who've died today. The city centre is shattered and so is my heart.

18:00 With my afternoon shopping trip sidelined, I have to use what's in the house for Tim's dinner. Two chickens, rice, potatoes and a few frozen vegetables. Cans of peaches and pears are our dessert. We have no bread and two boxes of milk. All stores and malls are closed and our local supermarket is in a devastating mess. I worry about food for a while then place it in God's hands.

23:30 I know I need to sleep so go to bed. I doze on and off but aftershocks rattle the house every 15 minutes or so.

04:30 I give up the battle and go downstairs to make tea for Kevin and coffee for myself. At the same time I dig the bread-maker out and dump ingredients into it.

06:00 Inspect the bread and see I forgot the yeast. I was the same after the September earthquake. My mind turned to mush and I struggled to remember simple things. I toss the bread away and head out with Kevin. Civil Defence requested that people stay home but we keep to back roads. The city is still, eerie and quiet as we drive along the edge of town and through the suburbs. The damage is overwhelming. Roads are cracked and sunk, homes destroyed, buildings shattered, cars crushed. I record the damage with photographs and a heavy heart.

Looking back, the September earthquake was more frightening physically but the emotional effects of the February quake were devastating. Although I'd only lived in Christchurch for five years at the time, I'd made it my home, a city I loved and cared for deeply. With that in mind, I wrote the following piece in early March.

My Shattered City by Debbie Roome

One minute.

That's all it took to shatter my city.

It was an average day, people going about their normal daily business: children at school, friends meeting for lunch, coffee shops crowded, streets busy, buskers entertaining.

Then it started; a rumble and a shake as the earth flexed its muscles. People stopped and looked at each other. Was it just a tremor?

The answer came as the motion accelerated violently, vibrating and shaking. Screams split the air punctuating the roar of falling bricks and crashing concrete. Homes broke in two, buildings collapsed, towers teetered and dust filled lungs. As the shaking continued, liquefaction erupted, silt burst to the surface and murky rivers flooded streets. Pipes twisted, roads cracked, tarmac distorted andpaving sunk. High above the suburbs, cliff faces cracked and boulders tumbled, crushing, destroying.

Oh God, where are You? How can this be happening?

For a terrible moment the city froze, 400,000 people in shocked limbo. Then terror unleashed itself. Sirens shrieked, buildings groaned, people wailed, scrabbling at rubble where loved ones had stood a moment earlier. The injured limped to open areas, blood streaming, features twisted in pain.

God is our refuge and strength, an ever-present help in trouble. Therefore we will not fear, though the earth give way and the mountains fall into the heart of the sea.

In the space of a minute, people's lives were irrevocably changed. Landscapes shifted, hills rose, buildings fell, dreams shattered. A violent monster wreaked havoc in our midst. Images of devastation and death were seared in minds, and brutal loss was burned in hearts forever.

After the wind there was an earthquake, but the Lord was not in the earthquake. After the earthquake came a fire, but the Lord was not in the fire. And after the fire came a gentle whisper.

One minute:
185 dead
Countless injured
100,000 homes damaged
10,000 homes destroyed
Infrastructures shattered
One third of the CBD ruined
Towers toppled
Famous icons broken
Businesses destroyed
Schools annihilated
Security lost

The city is left in ruins, its gate is battered to pieces ... the earth is broken up, the earth is split asunder, the earth is violently shaken. The earth reels like a drunkard.

Oh Lord, our hearts are broken at this terrible thing that has befallen our city. Memories are woven amongst the ruins of places where we worked ... and worshiped ... and played. Many of these places have become tombs and remind us that loved ones no longer stand by our sides. The loss of so many lives – people of every age, people from many nations - has brought us to our knees. Have mercy on us as we mourn as a nation, as we join hands with each other, our humanity binding us together. Remind us that this too shall pass ... and give us courage as we rise up and rebuild.

And the Lord whispered and said, "I will never leave you, nor forsake you."

One minute.

That's all it took.

Chapter Nine – The Impact of the 22nd February

The 22nd February earthquake deeply impacted every single person who was in Christchurch at the time – as well as millions of people outside of the city. Everyone who experienced the shaking and aftermath had a story to tell in the days and weeks that followed. The one recorded here gives a glimpse into the level of shock, pain and horror that Christchurch residents experienced ... as well as the hope that gave them strength to carry on in the days that followed.

My Earthquake Experience by Dee Bowers

Tues 22nd February 2011

8:30am

My morning started with a work team meeting which included a praise and worship time during which we say this song - it became a lifeline for me.

And That My Soul Knows Very Well
Darlene Zschech and Russell Fragar

You make Your face to shine on me
And that my soul knows very well
You lift me up, I'm cleansed and free
And that my soul knows very well

When mountains fall, I'll stand
By the power of Your hand

And in Your heart of hearts I'll dwell
And that my soul knows very well

Joy and strength each day I find
And that my soul knows very well
Forgiveness, hope, I know is mine
And that my soul knows very well

Around 9am

There was a 3.1 jolt that unnerved me for some reason and that 'on edge' feeling seemed to stay with me throughout the morning.

12.30pm

My friend Jane and I met at my office and we decided to pop downstairs to the Tasty Tucker for a catch up coffee. We chose a table at the back of the room and against the wall (this would prove to be a good choice) and settled in to have a good chat.

No concept of time

I was actually sharing about a significant experience of a spiritual nature when the whole room began to shake. It felt like we just sat and stared wide-eyed at each other for the first few seconds or so before we had any response at all.

We were just about to move when everything seemed to explode around us. The roof came crashing down and masonry flew in all directions. The noise was deafening and there was an incredible force that impacted our whole bodies. As the shaking subsided and dust filled our lungs we emerged from our stupor and reacted.

There were awful sounds all around, agonised moans and screams. I grabbed Jane's hand and remember glancing at my feet and seeing my handbag in the rubble. The logical part of my brain kicked in and my thought was *I need that, my mobile is in there.* I ripped it out of its position and we picked our way through the debris and around the back of the food counters towards the front door. I felt like I was in a time warp and every movement I made was somehow disconnected from my numb mind. Somehow I had become automated, robotic.

I was behind my friend Jane as she ducked under a fallen piece of metal sheeting and made her way out the front door and onto the street. I was about to do the same when my path was blocked by a piece of the ceiling that had been moved to get to the injured. In front of me I saw a lady pinned under the 'V' of the caved in roof, I felt completely helpless as there was no way to get to her. Then out of the corner of my eye I saw another lady crawling from under the mess of wooden beams and fallen bricks in the middle of the room – I said, "here, take my hand" and pulled her towards me. She expressed her need to get to her partner who was back on the other side of the room – where I had just come from. I heard someone shout 'the back door is open' so I led her back, she reunited with her partner and they made their way out.

I was hesitant to leave - everything in me wanted to help who ever I could, but I also knew the logical thing to do was get out of the building. Someone screeched 'phone 111' and so I tried but of course could not get through. I was about to step around and try and help elsewhere when a voice bellowed, "All able bodied people, get out, we don't need more injuries." (I learnt later that the police and others had already arrived to help – amazing.) With that I took myself out through the back entrance.

I stepped out into the sunlight and made my way to our office car park. There I saw my work mates gathered, the relief was incredible, a moment of joy in a world gone crazy - everybody was okay. There was lots of hugging, crying and then we huddled in a circle and started to pray. Suddenly the second big aftershock jolted our senses, but somehow it wasn't as bad as we were all together. My colleagues fussed over me, concerned about the wound I

114

had to my lip and the shock symptoms I was displaying. They wrapped me in a borrowed jacket and consoled and comforted. I will always be so grateful for this outpouring of love and selflessness from them.

My next thought was for my family and extended family I had staying with me at the time. This was closely followed by the need to let Jane know that I had got out of the back of the building, I knew she was safe but she had no idea where I had disappeared to and I guessed she would be frantic with concern. The texts started flying and we all supported each other as we tried to get messages to our loved ones – near impossible as we all experienced.

A man came to where we were congregated and asked if anybody was injured. He took one look at me and said "you're coming with me." I exchanged a look with the fine young man who was our leader that day and he gave me my mobile and said "Go Dee, you need medical attention, just let us know where you are. We'll be alright, we'll stick together here."

The man marched me round to the triage that had been set up in record time at the Spotlight car park – amazingly organised in such a small timeframe. There were policemen, army personnel, doctors and nurses attending to badly hurt patients, pharmacy staff bringing out bandages and taking down names, etc., people comforting and talking to the injured, others retrieving foam mattresses and blankets to be used - everybody pulling together as one.

I was supported by a lovely young lady, who led me to a seat, draped a foil insulator around me followed by a warm blanket, all the time making reassuring conversation – at last the uncontrollable shivering in my body began to subside. Then wonders upon wonders I was enveloped in an emotional hug from my friend Jane (who was sporting a bandage to stem the bleeding from a wound to the back of her head). Just another moment of joy as we reconnected and knew for sure that we were both okay.

We sat holding hands, comforting each other, praying for the many around us who were in deep pain and suffering. Three times the helicopter swooped down into the car park and took away the severely injured. Trauma seemed to be everywhere, but peppered amongst it were these beautiful moments of human kindness – smiles, hugs, soft words of comfort and encouragement. We grieved as we learnt that most of the injured were from the Tasty Tucker Coffee shop – the building we had been in - and that one person had not made it out alive.

I remember quietly humming to myself the tune of the song we had sung that morning; 'and that my soul knows very well' as my numb mind began to return to some semblance of thought. I pulled out my phone and began the frantic task of trying to get hold of my precious husband, Craig. I had been told of the devastation in the CBD and remembered that he was at a meeting in the town hall that morning. I was unsure of his whereabouts at the time of the quake. I also knew that my children were finishing school at 12 o'clock that day due to the teacher's involvement at the same meeting. Miraculously I got a call through to my home and was reassured by my brother-in-law that although everyone was in shock, they were all alright and that my children had phoned in to say they were safe. I kept the details of my situation to a minimum and felt it sufficient to say that I was doing okay – I think we spoke for about thirty seconds! Finally a text came through from Craig to say he was safe but obviously deeply concerned about me as he had got word from my work colleagues that I was injured. In our broken communication we arranged that Craig would try and get to me at the triage but I still didn't know where exactly he was coming from. I managed to get word of my whereabouts to my work colleagues as well.

As the controlled chaos continued around me, tears burned my eyes, the wound I had to my lip was gently cleaned and dressed, the numbness began to subside, and a surreal calmness seemed to settle over me. There was a real sense of Jesus' presence right there with us in the middle of all this pain and confusion.

Around 4:15pm

The familiar sound of a text coming through 'Hi love, coming down Brougham Street, traffic not moving much, are you able to walk, can you meet me' my reply text 'Yes, corner of Brougham and Durham Street South.' I hugged the few people who remained at the triage thanking them for their amazing kindness, happy to know my dear friend Jane had been taken off to the medical centre to have her head stitched; I made my way through the bumpy streets that were by this time swimming with silt and water from liquefaction. I reached the arranged meeting place and decided to walk further up the road. As I passed shell-shocked people all trying to get somewhere we exchanged sad smiles and greetings of "how you doing." I had gone a couple of blocks and I sensed this voice saying, 'turn around go back to where you said you would meet Craig!' I obeyed!

Thank you Lord that I did! As I reached the spot I heard this heartfelt cry "Loooooovvve" from the other side of the street! Suffice it to say we stopped traffic that day (albeit slow moving traffic!) as I ran across the street to get to the love of my life! I clambered into our van and proceeded to have a complete melt down. My husband lovingly held my hand, comforting me as he continued to negotiate through the traffic, both of us desperate to get home. As it turned out Craig had gone back to Rangiora where he teaches and we thank God he had left the CBD. However he had experienced a three hour drive through some of the most devastated areas of Christchurch, all the while frantic with concern for all of us.

It was okay now – we were together!

Around 5:00pm
Finally we got home and what a great reunion that was – everybody was together – at last! I think just about every emotion possible was felt as we looked at each other in shocked bewilderment. It was a long time before we could really express how we felt and share our individual stories.

Within an hour of getting home and in the days to follow, we had to kick in to practical mode. We fetched water, boiled water, made sure we had enough food on hand; moved mattresses downstairs, the men dug the dunny. We helped neighbours and family, made numerous phone calls

118

and dealt with the emotion of hearing harrowing story after story, realising we were not alone in our experience.

That disconnected, automated, robotic existence seemed to be there again. However, in the background was always the gentle tune 'and that my soul knows very well' the sense of Jesus holding my hand, walking through the valley with me, His rod and His staff comforting me.

Thursday 24th February, 4:00pm
My mum took me off to the doctor to check out my lip and light headedness I was experiencing. As I explained what had happened the Doctor and nurses gasped in horror at the realisation that their good friend and colleague had been in the same building as me. As we discussed it we realised she was the lady I had seen caught under caved-in roof. With tears in their eyes they let me know her spinal cord had been severed and she was in a very bad way. I felt devastated and very sad for their pain. Then another

emotion hit me – guilt – I got out relatively unscathed and she was paralysed. They said it was good to hear a firsthand account of what happened as they had been unsure of the full story. This brought a little comfort to a heart-breaking situation.

As the post earthquake days have turned to weeks this incredible paradox has remained the common theme for me – the agony for all the suffering and the praising God for the many, many miracle stories including my own.

There are so many unanswered questions but as I heard someone say recently – "this was not an act of God; this was an imperfect world doing what an imperfect world does." The comforting word from a stranger, the unexpected help from a neighbour, the touching acts of kindness we see all around us – these are the 'acts of God'– this is the HOPE I carry in my heart as we go about allowing the Lord to help us repair our broken lives, adapt to our new normal and together build a beautiful future for the next generation.

Thy Kingdom come, Thy will be done on earth as it is in heaven.

'And that my soul knows very well.'

Chapter Ten – Experiences of the 22nd February

Christchurch Earthquake Memories by Ian Graham

It's 12:50pm on Tuesday 22nd February 2011. I'm just back from a lunchtime walk round the block and it's sunny and warm. I have a meeting at 1pm and am sitting at my desk talking to a workmate about, of all things, smoked eel. There is a small shake and I have time to think, *we haven't had one of those for a while*. But this wasn't an aftershock. Instead, the ground started heaving, convulsing violently. I dive under my desk, head down. I look up, by now scared and think, *this has to stop, please stop*. The noise is something different, sometimes you can hear an earthquake coming – a deep rumbling sound coming towards you – but this time, nothing, no warning. The building shakes, some pieces of equipment fall from benches.

Then it stops, there's a moment of silence like time is standing still. Then, almost together, everyone returns to their senses and heads for the door. As we are standing in the car park, an aftershock hits. The building rumbles and it is as if the hundred or so cars in the car park each have one person on either side, trying to rock them as much as they can.

We talk and theorise that this earthquake was centred a lot closer than the September one, maybe even right beneath us. Thoughts then turn to heading for home. The traffic isn't that bad, the roads are fine. There is silty water coming up through the grass just north of Belfast, but that is about all. I think it isn't as bad as it was in September.

I get home and Kay isn't here so decide to head for Miriama's school. I don't get far before I see Kay's car coming the other way. We are all safe and hug each other on the driveway. A quick check round the house shows no damage, maybe one of the cracks in the driveway has got a bit wider.

Then I turn the TV on. News bulletins are on each of the main channels. We usually watch TV One news, but this time TV3 is more up to date. The reality sinks in. Last time, in September, we were lucky. That earthquake struck at 4:35am, when most people (me not included, I was just about to go fishing!) were tucked up in bed. But this time, it's different. There are images of blood-stained people being helped to safety, and of a Samoan man lifting fallen blocks of concrete in a desperate search for anyone buried underneath what remains of a coffee shop in City Mall. Two major buildings have collapsed: the Pyne Gould building on Cambridge Terrace and the CTV building on Madras Street. There is a worker at Pyne Gould, his shirt ripped, wheeling a bin towards the building so he can climb on it to help someone trapped inside. A lady is rescued from the roof by a fireman. On the lawn outside, the injured are laid down awaiting ambulances. A floor has also collapsed at The Press building and there are people trapped there too.

Then the image that really brings it home; the Cathedral, the centrepiece of the city. The spire has toppled forwards and lies in ruins. In September, the Cathedral stood firm, a sign of hope. But this time, it's gone. A woman sits by a window in the side face of the Cathedral awaiting rescue; they get her out.

Pictures of devastation continue. The CTV building where we'd had marriage counselling on the top floor a year before, has been reduced to a pile of rubble; all that is left is the stairwell. And what's worse, it is on fire. Rescuers search desperately for survivors. There are reports a bus has been crushed by falling masonry. This too proves to be true. Surely not everyone got out of there.

Liquefaction, the forcing of water up through the ground caused by the weight of the buildings on top is reported and some suburbs to the south and east of the city are flooded. It's not just the water that's the problem; it's the silt it leaves behind. It covers everything, absolutely everything. All afternoon, evening and in to the night, these images continue. The reality is now sinking in. This time there will be fatalities, many fatalities.

My pastor, Andy, phones us to check we are okay. I ask if there is any news of other church members and there is - news of the worst kind. Isaac, son of our children's pastor, was in the CTV building and hasn't been heard from since. He is a trainee cameraman there. My thoughts flash to the time he helped us out during an Alpha course. One night, the DVD player remote was nowhere to be found, rendering the machine next to useless. Isaac happened to be there practicing with the music group. He went home and minutes later turned up with a DVD player, remote, and everything we needed. Now we need to pray for him, as there is near certainty he is buried somewhere in the CTV building ruins.

Then there is a feeling of guilt that we weren't hit. A big aftershock hits, a 5.9, but that is all. It is quiet, nowhere near as many aftershocks as in September. Has such a disaster really happened only 30 kilometres away? We sleep very little that night, not because of the aftershocks, but because we are in a daze. Disasters only happen somewhere else, not on our doorstep; except this one has.

It's Wednesday 23rd February now and the rescuers from our country and those that have flown in from Australia are still pulling survivors from the wreckage. The first fatalities are also confirmed. The day passes in an almost unreal state as we watch the drama play out on television. In the evening, there is finally something we can do to help. People made homeless in Christchurch need somewhere to stay, and our church has been earmarked as that somewhere. Rangiora Baptist Church is to become the Rangiora Welfare Centre and it must be ready to receive several hundred people by 8pm. An appeal goes out for bedding and food, and we are inundated. We make a plan then lay out 200 beds on the auditorium floor and the stage. The girls follow behind making the beds neat and as welcoming as they can. Toys are placed on the children's beds.

It's Thursday now, and no more survivors have been found, only bodies. At 5pm we are told to get ready to receive 400 people from an overcrowded welfare centre in Christchurch. It's all hands on deck, but only about 40 turn up. Afterwards, we stand outside. It is a lovely late summer's evening. We comment it just doesn't seem real that such a disaster is playing out only 30kilometres away.

This number of evacuees we receive steadily rises to about 100 during Friday. I go to help on Saturday morning, ferrying the sick from the AMI centre to the church to have some breakfast, and taking some from the church up to the AMI centre for showers. These poor people want to talk about it, but most can barely string a sentence together. They are like stunned mullets.

We work in shifts with the Civil Defence people during the week, doing what we can to make these people's lives a little bit easier. The following Friday, our welfare centre is closed. There is now enough space for these homeless people in other centres in Christchurch. But they don't want to go. Several say they have felt loved at our church, something they hadn't felt at other centres. But, the authorities make their decision and the people leave us, off to more uncertainty.

Here, it is still quiet, much quieter than it was after the September earthquake. It is like the pressure built up has now been released in devastating fashion

Damage Caused by the February Earthquake by Isaac Noble

When the February earthquake struck I was in the middle of the northern motorway doing pre re-seal repairs. We had just stopped as the boss had arrived. As the earthquake hit the boss commented on the cars stopping on the road but I was more worried about the gum trees above that were waving wildly and it was quite frightening as I know they fall fairly
easily.

I called Hannah and she said she was safe, sitting under a table at uni. We secured the job site where we had been working and received instructions to head towards Lyttelton. It was slow progress and when we reached the eastern suburbs, we stopped frequently to pull cars out of sink holes. That first day we got as far as Sumner.

The second day was spent in the Ferrymead area. I worked 7am to 6pm
every day that week and cleared tons of silt from
Ferrymead Village and Pacific Park. I remember using a 5

ton digger to try and pull a car out of the silt and it wouldn't budge. On

other days I used a 14 ton digger to remove silt. On Mackenzie Ave a massive hole had opened as a result of the liquefaction and we used 18 14-ton truck loads of gravel to fill it.

In the following weeks we worked on roads in the Sumner, Redcliffs and hill areas. The road near New World in Redcliffs had lifted by as much as a foot in places and the road between Redcliffs and Sumner was very badly damaged. We repaired a road on the hills and after what I saw, I would never buy a house up there. The gap in the tarmac was only about 15 centimetres but when we opened up the crack, the split was much wider.

Five months later we were still repairing roads around the city and every time an aftershock of more than 5.0 magnitude struck, it would cause fresh liquefaction and the resulting silt would damage the repairs we had just done.

Though it may be years away I am looking forward to Christchurch being rebuilt to her former glory with smooth roads and chlorine free water in all the suburbs.

Choices by Lois Farrow

Our friend, Christy, from Korea has been in Christchurch with a group of children for a month. They will leave on Friday and we plan a farewell lunch in town while the children are at school. Shall we meet Monday or Tuesday? We decide on Monday, so at 11am on 21st February 2011 my former neighbour, Gina, and I are waiting at Ballantynes corner. Gina is freaked by the Ballantynes windows, huge plate glass windows with large cracks criss-crossing them, taped up with what appears to be sellotape. They were damaged in the September and December earthquakes. Waiting bus passengers stand close to the windows, but Gina makes sure we stand well away. They don't look safe, she says. I agree, but it's been over five months since the September earthquake, and the Boxing Day shake has been and gone, so what are the chances of another one? We are trying to pretend life is back to normal, but uncertainty is present.

Christy and her friend arrive, and we stroll along Cashel Mall to the Dux de Lux for a delicious lunch. Our time is precious. We take our time around the Arts Centre as they consider gifts to take home. We return to Ballantynes corner where I say my goodbyes as the three of them head for a bus to Riccarton for further shopping, and I walk down Colombo Street to South City. When I have what I need, I walk back to St. Asaph Street to catch my Halswell bus and am home by 3.30 pm.

Next day, 22nd February, I am home at 12.51pm when the big one strikes. I brace myself against the kitchen bench and hold on. My husband comes from the bathroom where he was trying to fix a blocked drain.

"This feels similar to the September one," we say, stunned. Once again our house shows no signs of damage, and we are grateful, but the power is off. As the afternoon proceeds we continue to be rocked by strong aftershocks.

"This is much worse than September," we say My brother rings from Auckland to see how we are and to relay the unfolding tragedy reported on TV. There is terrible damage in the city and people have been killed. This is much worse. There is not much for us to do except wait it out. Our neighbourhood is fine, but it is clear that the rest of the city is in a terrible state. Power is restored about 10pm, only nine hours out this time; it was twelve hours in September. Once again we don't lose our water.

Next morning we rush for The Press to get the news, grateful for their courage in printing in spite of extraordinarily difficult circumstances. As the days unfold we watch the news and hear friends' stories. Because we have water we have friends in to our place for showers and laundry. We help clean up in friends' houses on badly damaged Huntsbury hill. I can't believe someone wants to go back in their house when the windows have slipped, bricks have fallen off, and house frames are twisted and buckled. Facebook sports the latest photos of 'our new plywood house' or 'our backyard dunny.'

My brother comes from Auckland and we spend a few days helping Grace church in New Brighton where they are running a drop-in centre. We do some visiting and

129

meal delivery for them, finding our way around buckled roads. People are doing their best. It helps when the sun shines and they can sit outside, and forget the mess inside. Armies of people shift silt. Many people face uncertainty and mess for months or years to come.

I still don't know if Ballantynes windows fell out or stayed in place. Early photos showed Cashel Mall covered in rubble, with dust rising and chaos everywhere. It is nearly three months before I see an aerial shot of the section of Colombo Street where I walked, footpath piled high with rubble, squashed and mangled buses on the street.

It still seems surreal to be carrying on with life as normal, when half the city is in such devastation. But of course things are not really normal, the traffic is chaotic, businesses are closed or opening in different places, friends are affected and we are all involved in helping in various ways.

I missed the chaos by a day through our choice to go to town on Monday. Many people missed death by a whisker, and were much closer to it than I was, and I feel for all those who lost loved ones that day. It's a freaky thought that the little choices we make each day are sometimes a matter of life or death.

Our Shattered Symbol by Shirley Shelton

A
7.1
4.9.2010
0435
A
hit
deep
down
below
ground
Violent
Shaking
No water
No power
No sewage
Earthquake
Deaths – nil

A	Liquefaction	A
6.3	Stunned faces	6.3
1251	Frazzled nerves	1420

22.2.11 many aftershocks 13.6.11
Our Cathedral stood proud and tall
Buildings, infrastructure & homes
destroyed.   Streets like river beds.
Munted, cordons, curfews, red-zone, drop-zone & heroes. Another earthquake, in
day-light – 181 deaths. Homeless, jobless, confused people and unbelievably the
spire came down.
Our beautiful city of
Christchurch, munted!
Two earthquakes
one June day
fear & despair
tear moistened
rubble mountains
demolishion crews
vacant spaces.
Visionary plans
a new Central City
revive hopes & dreams.
Do we need a new
Symbol?

Chapter Eleven - More Stories from the 22nd February

Preservation by Ann Finnemore

February 22nd 2011 was the day we were to have our roof
fixed from the September quake. However, it was raining
so I did not expect to see the roofers. On the journey home
from visiting friends, I stopped off at St Martin's New
World, (the docket states the time of paying at 12:44) then
headed home to Heathcote Valley, driving along the Port
Hills Road. Just before the flyover to Lyttelton the car
became an out-of-control monster and threw me to the side
of the road. Self preservation kicked in and I put on the
brakes and jumped out the car. The road left my feet,
another shudder, I screamed. The driver behind me had
also jumped out of his car. He opened his arms wide and I
ran into them sobbing and asking if he had been in the
September one. The poor man said it was his first
earthquake and he was from Australia. After reassurance
both ways we continued our separate journeys very, very
slowly.

My house was only a minute away, but the road
was moving and shuddering. Something ran along the road
the Port Hills Road. At first I thought was a rabbit - it was
running so fast you could hardly see that it was a cat.
When I got home my husband was outside with neighbours
and they were all supporting each other. Then another
quake struck, a 5.9. It was terrifying.

Our house suffered damage even though it was
only 18 months old and nothing was left inside any of the
cupboards. Like most people we had a smashed

smorgasbord of food – wine, flour, oil, jam, fish sauce, china and glass.

Where was my husband when it struck? Yes, you guessed right. On the toilet. He said he thought he was going to be hit by the sink as it rushed towards him! Little did we know it would be sometime before such a luxury as a toilet would be available again.

Later on we were to learn that Heathcote Valley recorded one of the greatest ever ground accelerations in the world and that the simultaneous vertical and horizontal ground movement made it nearly impossible for buildings to survive intact.

We left to join our family at Mount Pleasant and arrived to find two much-traumatised grandchildren and an American visitor who was staying with my son and his wife. We set up a makeshift safety zone on their deck. The children were shaking so much they could not get warm so we piled blanket after blanket on them and wrapped them up like cocoons. They had been at school at Redcliffs and had witnessed the rock face falling and heard the terrified screams of children around them. Each shake bought new terrors but finally the children settled and waited for the return of all the missing adults.

Our son was out with his sister, (the children's mother) checking and warning people to get out of their homes. The side of the road at Mount Pleasant was slipping and the houses below were sitting on the edge. Their Dad was on the other side of town as was their aunty. Six hours later they all arrived home safe but their stories of the journey back to Mount Pleasant were like a disaster movie. They told of wading through silt and water, going past cars that had slid into massive holes, and riding a bike with no brakes, kindly loaned by a young teenager on

134

finding out that aunty still had a long way to go. There were also broken roads and bridges down. As my sister said a few weeks later, with so many of us living in Christchurch, the family in the UK were fully prepared to hear bad news. All I could say was we were being looked after!

Update after February 22, 2011 by Janette Busch

"There's been another big earthquake in Christchurch; 6.3; there are injuries."

Incredibly, I was once again away from Christchurch when this earthquake hit; attending a conference in Auckland. Instinctively, I reached for my mobile phone and joined the surge of others from Christchurch to the foyer. Instantly, I was thrown into the unwanted familiarity of a maelstrom of confusion, anguish and despair as I tried to contact my family, and the trauma of being away from the city I love in her time of need overwhelmed me (tears come as I write this).

None of us could make cell phone contact but then a cleaner working there realised why we were all so stressed and told us to go outside as there was no reception there, even in normal times.

My first contact was from Andrew, who was working temporarily in Wellington. By then he and Catherine had been in contact with each other, so I knew my family was fine.

Remembering from the September earthquake, I took the opportunity to go to the airport with others to get my flight changed. As we travelled the colleague on my right (who was not from Christchurch) said, "You seem very calm." I took a deep breath, waited and then said, "I am a Christian." There was no response so I continued, speaking slowly, "I believe I hear God saying to me 'All will be well.' I continued, "I don't know what I will be facing when I get home, but since He said that, it is enough for me."

That afternoon my son-in-law Shaun drove heroically through roads packed with panicking people leaving the city, to check on the security of my house. Andrew caught an early evening ferry from Wellington to Picton and drove through the night to Christchurch, arriving in the early hours of the morning. After a sleepless night at a friend's place in Auckland, I arrived home at lunch time.

I don't have anyone close to me who was killed and am grateful for that.

My house suffered more damage but now that all sorts of emergency repairs have been done it is battered but liveable. Once again I must wait for a decision to be made about its future.

My personal struggle after the earthquakes has been trying to explain to others how I was as much traumatised by not being in Christchurch as they were in being here, but in a different way. I too have felt and been negatively affected by the ongoing aftershocks. It is hard when my experience is dismissed with the words, "You weren't here so you don't understand how I feel" when I try to share with others how I am also affected. This makes me think I have no right to feel as I do.

Like many others in Christchurch, I suffer from what we call "earthquake brain" with its struggle to find words when speaking; the forgetfulness, the lack of concentration and motivation and the huge energy, both emotional and physical, needed to deal with the ongoing stressful and frustrating situations arising from living in a damaged city.

When I flew to the North Island for short visit a couple of months after the earthquake, tears flooded my eyes as the plane took off; "I am abandoning my city in her time of need," I told myself. On coming home, as soon as I saw the lights of Christchurch as the plane made its descent the tears returned – I was home.

This is my city, my future. I cannot abandon her. She will rise again and I want to be part of that.

Another Wake-Up call by Kay Graham

Living out in Woodend as we do, we didn't feel all of the aftershocks, especially once they declined in frequency and magnitude. Gradually we learnt to ignore even those which did make themselves felt. Ironically, I was sitting at my computer working on this piece when that situation abruptly changed again. Although the 22nd February aftershock was a lesser magnitude, it scared me far more than the 7.1 we had in September. Whether that is because I was awake, because I was alone, or because I had already seen the aftermath of a big quake I'm not sure, but I was far less sensible this time. Instead of taking shelter, I grabbed the house keys and bolted for the garden. Even when it was over, I stood out on the driveway shaking, not wanting to go back into the house. A friendly wave from an elderly gentlemen at the end of the road made me feel much better – a little bit of friendliness can go a long way.

When I did go back in, I set about finding out how Ian and Miri got through the aftershock. It was a frightening time, especially as the telephone lines were out of action to begin with; but eventually I got through to Miri's school in Rangiora. The receptionist informed me parents were already arriving to pick up their children, who were unhurt, though understandably frightened.

Knowing Miri was alright, I decided to delay going to collect her until I had made sure my husband was unhurt. Several attempts later, my call to his workplace was connected. One of his colleagues assured me they were all fine, and that many of them were already on their way home.

The entire school was out in the playground when I arrived. Miri spotted me immediately and ran straight into my arms before starting to cry. She was very distressed, screaming every time there was an aftershock and was too scared to sleep in her own bed. We installed her on a camp bed in our room for several nights, until she recovered her sense of humour. Within a couple of days, she was back to her normal self.

It will obviously take a lot longer for Christchurch to recover from this aftershock. For now, we are taking each day as it comes. Ian helped out at the Welfare Centre which was set up at Rangiora Baptist Church; Miri and I spent time volunteering to spread the word about the Earthquake Support Service. The tears came every so often when I thought about the disaster which has hit our beautiful city, but I tried to be practical and help where I could. One thing was certain – the petrol and food shortages would pass, in time destroyed buildings would be rebuilt, but our lives would never be quite the same again.

Earthquake Diary - Dave Palmer

It's Tuesday, February 22, 2011, early in the afternoon. I am awake but in bed after a night of taxi driving. I have just read, again, the passage in Matthew's gospel where Jesus speaks of wars, famines and earthquakes – which he calls 'the beginning of birth pangs.'

The room shakes with a muscular violence. Stuff crashes. Is this one bigger than September 4? I was in the taxi for that one, so comparison is impossible. This one is shorter, so I decide it's probably not as bad this time.

I dress, wander up the drive and ask a neighbour how she is. She's shaking, but okay. Cars stream both ways, moving at a snail's pace but not stopping. Water and silt pour out of the flats next door. I feel both guilty and helpless as the radio reports on the destruction, injuries and the first deaths in the city centre.

I check on Nigel who has cerebral palsy. He tells me he's very frightened and asks me to stay overnight. I baulk. I don't want to handle his needs and demands. I leave, but tell him I will come back to say yes or no. Two hours later, I return, ready to take him to my place. There is no power or water, but we will cope somehow. But he's not there. Someone else came to get him.

The mobile network is working, very slowly, and I smile at the value of old technology as I plug in the old corded phone. Sam, my son, calls to offer me a bed at his home in Rangiora, where there is very little damage. I feel guilty about leaving my neighbours, but not guilty enough. The hot shower beckons. I stay overnight and come back to the city each day.

Taxi work has dropped virtually to nil. But I decide that I owe it to my boss to at least try. It's Thursday and there is no dispatch service. I cruise for six hours, getting one job. Saturday night is slightly better. We have voice dispatch and I take home about a third of my normal fare. And that's with eighty percent of the fleet not working. Again, I feel guilty. I have chosen to work rather than offer to help in some welfare capacity.

Rahel my neighbour and I shovel about twenty barrow-loads of silt from our driveway out to the road. She's strong and I'm impressed. Thirty-plus and single. I tell her someone's missing out on a very good catch.

What am I supposed to think about this earthquake? Sitting in the taxi doing nothing gives me time to reflect. But it feels wrong to reflect. The rescue and welfare teams, and thousands of others in their neighbourhoods, are doing the appropriately-named 'acts of God.' I decide that Job's comforters got it right when they just sat with him silently for a week. 'Where is God in all this' can wait.

But not for long. Ken Ring speaks, and everybody listens. March 20 is a probability, he says, give or take a few days, 8 to 9 on the Richter scale. Others have also spoken of a catastrophic quake in March. Back in October, one person I know very well predicted a major shake in February. 'Prepare for a big one, with tsunami, in March', she tells me. In the first hour of March, fear blackens me. I strongly feel I may have three weeks to live. I talk a lot to God and make efforts to get myself right with Him. I'm also praying that Ken Ring will be wrong, because if he's right, he will surely have lots of disciples hanging on his every word.

At the end of the March 18th memorial service a young woman comes up to me and says she feels strongly prompted to tell me how much God loves me. She says she's been praying and feeling this prompting throughout the service. I think the Holy Spirit is in her words, and I'm blown away.

April has arrived, and all the predictions of a big one in March have come to nothing. I can't help feeling hugely relieved.

Created Perfect by Ruth Linton

Created perfect, world
Of vibrant colours, variety of form,
Abundant fruit, fragrant blooms
Friendly beasts of land, sea and sky
Intended as a flawless, fitting home
For the Divine creators highest frame—
Male and female human-kind.

Pristine splendour fades:
The sinful fall of man
Brings blighted crops, aggressive beasts.
Sorrow, pain and death increase.
Humanity revolts and drifts away
From their extravagant Creator.
Eternal hope is gone.

Turmoil fills the world!
Six thousand years have passed.
Perfection scarred and ravaged by a world-wide flood
Unwillingly subjected to enforced decline -
Pollution, greed and reckless use -
Now groans and travails as it dreams
Of Eden's glory to reclaim.

Tectonic plates lurch,
Crust cracks! Earth contorts,
Bears down , pushes, pants, bursts forth
Panorama of destruction—
Toppled towers, eroded hills.
Liquefaction, oozing water, muck and dust
Engulfs unsuspecting man.

Where will it end?
Earth groans and travails as it awaits
The revelation of the sons of God
Whose hearts are knit with their Redeemer's plan,
Who eagerly anticipate His imminent return.
He will release the earth, and free it from the curse
Into the glorious liberty
Intended for the sons of God.

Shaken and Stirred by Beth Walker

Beth lives in Auckland but spent a month in Christchurch over Christmas 2010 and New Year 2011. The letter below is fictional but expresses her feelings and experiences whilst in the city and is also based on the hours she spent following news reports.

Dear Stevie,

How are you? In your corner of the world you might not have heard much about the awful earthquake Christchurch had in February so I'll try to fill in the gaps. It was as though a madman shook the city, flicked things up and threw them down, some of them landing in different places.

The CBD was trashed and nearly 200 people died. Luckily I was at home and none of my family or friends were injured. About 60,000 people left the city. Many have returned and while more will, others won't.

Emergency services worked around the clock and saved hundreds. I think of the search and rescue teams, and medical staff who treated injuries, shock and pain. Security is still a problem in some areas and the CBD is off limits.

Businesses have moved to different places and many schools are sharing campuses. The ground and roads are full of cracks, bumps and silt deposits from liquefaction. People have to sort out new ways to go anywhere, everywhere. It's hard for us all.

Countless homes lost some or all basic services – power, water, communications and sewage – for hours, weeks or months. It will be a long time before the sewage system is fully restored. Many people use portaloos in the street, while others set up a toilet in their garden. Some have to put their mess in plastic bags to be collected. Also we've learned a new way to do washing – hang it on the line, wait for rain and hope it's clean.

Almost everything's changed and we need to work out how to do even the most basic stuff. It's as though we're in a battle, except that no one's firing weapons at us. On top of all that, the constant aftershocks keep people stretched and stressed out. Some are at breaking point and dread sleeping or showering in case there's yet another aftershock. Domestic violence has increased.

Things could be worse, however. People brought us food and water from all over the place and most supermarkets reopened soon after the quake. Our basic needs are being met and in some surprising ways.

Life here will be an uphill slog for a long time. We'll pull through somehow, and I'm surviving.

Please think of us,
Chris

My Civil Defence Hair Do by Karen Price

I'm a hairdresser by profession and the 22nd February 2011 was my day off. I was in the salon in St Albans having my hair done – colour and foils. Just before the earthquake, the foils were taken out and I was on my way to the basin when the earthquake struck. It was pandemonium and after the shaking settled, silt and water started bubbling up in the car park. Everyone was upset and said we needed to get out of there before our cars got stuck in the silt. "Hang on," I said, "Can we just rinse my hair off first." We went back to the basin but there was no water and no power. We looked in the toilet cistern but there was no way to get water from there so we tried the fridge. There was some Just Juice and a half bottle of milk in there. My colleague poured this over my hair and scrunched it in, trying to remove the bleach and colour. It turned out as a multi-coloured creamy mass on my head as there wasn't enough liquid to rinse the bleach out.

With a towel around my head, I climbed into my car and decided to head to my mother's house in Hornby. It took me two hours just to get to the end of Bealey Ave and another 90 minutes from there to Hornby. En route, the towel slipped off my shoulders and I felt like a freak sitting in my car. Every few minutes I pulled the sun visor down to check what I looked like in the mirror. It wasn't a pretty sight but no one in the nearby cars batted an eyelid. Everyone was in too much shock.

When I finally reached my mother's house, I rinsed the gunk off my hair and found it had turned bright orange – the same colour as Bob Parker's famous jacket! I decided it was the least of my worries with the tragedy that had befallen our city and left it as it was. Everybody who saw it commented that they liked my new look. The brightness faded after a few days to a strawberry blonde and I waited a month before redoing the colour.

Chapter Twelve – More Stories from Teens and Children

George's Story - age 9

I was at Redcliffs School, it was lunch time and I was in my class finishing some work that I hadn't finished when everyone else had. I was sitting at my desk which was furtherest away from the door, all on my own. Then I heard some rumbling then shaking and it got bigger and bigger. I knew it was a big earthquake and it was not going to be good. Suddenly the desks were flipping over on their sides on the floor. I had difficulty walking out and had to climb over them and as I went out the bookcase fell on top of me. I got out and I looked behind me and saw the biggest dust cloud ever! The cliffs had fallen down at the back of the school, I ran to the front playfield following everyone else, there was screaming all around. Then my sister Abbey found me. She cuddled me and Mum turned up 2-3 minutes later. No one in the school was injured, just a few scratches.

Where did the River Go by E-J McLennan age 15

We were sitting at the table, 12.51pm. It was lunch time on an ordinary Tuesday. All around Christchurch, people were eating lunch in cafes downtown, sitting outside in the warm sunshine or at school. We were oblivious to the impending disaster. Then the Earthquake hit. It happened so suddenly, violently and devastatingly that we will never forget it. As soon as it started I remember thinking, "no way, this can't be happening again.''I knew as we sat huddled under the table that there would be people dying in Christchurch. I saw the washing line bouncing up and down through the window, and everything crashing to the floor around us as the deep rumbling continued. Once the initial earthquake was over, we turned on the TV to see and hear the devastation more vividly than I could ever have imagined.

In the city there was chaos and confusion; people lost, trapped, terrified. Sirens wailed and our icon, the Cathedral, had crumbled. People were injured and dead. "I was in that building half an hour ago," Dad said, pointing to one which had been crushed. We were so lucky. After that, I walked into the kitchen and opened the cupboard; only to have all of the plates and glasses come flying out at me and smash on the floor. I got such a fright. It finally hit me what was going on and I burst into tears.

When we thought it was safe, Dad and I went to go check on people down the street. We were a few doors down when the 5.3 hit. I looked across to someone's driveway where the cars were bouncing up and down, the trees swaying, and the ground rippling beneath us. It was like something from a horror movie, twisted and terrifying. We ran back home and an hour or two later we packed our bags and left to stay with our family down in Southland.

We are now back in Christchurch. Although many things are back to normal, we will never be the same. The Avon is a muddy mess, with uprooted trees in the middle of it and no water. Where did the river go? I went into town with my family a couple days ago, and although it was sad to see so many buildings being demolished or gone altogether, that wasn't what hit me the most. It was how quiet it was, like a ghost town. Because essentially Christchurch isn't an area, a city, a group of buildings and suburbs. It's the people who live here that make it such a wonderful place. Think of all the people who have helped us since the earthquake. Rescue teams and the Red Cross, school fundraisers, the student army, our friends and family to name a few. We will miss our local shops, our icons, our hockey fields and most of all, the people who have died. Someday we will rebuild, repair and renew to make a safer city. Someday we will proudly tell our grandchildren of how brave we were, and how huge an earthquake can be. Someday the Avon will flow again.

A Strange Holiday by April McLennan – Age 13

February 22nd, 2011. Since my family home-schools, we were all at home and Dad had just come back for lunch, from a downtown appointment. As we sat down to our meal, the room started violently shaking, and of course our immediate reaction was "is this big"? And then, finding out it was, we dove under the table. I admit, in my head I was thinking about all those predictions of there being a huge 8 earthquake or something, and this felt like it. If the 7.1 crashed a tidal wave of emotions over my head, this one felt like a tsunami! Again, we texted friends to check if they were alright. When I received a text saying "The Cathedral's down, people dead," and we watched it on TV, my heart sank. But we were so glad Dad had got back from downtown and was completely okay, as was all the friends and everyone we had heard of so far.

As aftershocks continued to rattle everything and everyone, my two younger sisters were watching a movie on our portable DVD player while the rest of us checked on our neighbours and people in our area, and watched TV to find out what we were to do. Then, a couple of hours later, my Dad asked Mum, E-J and I what we thought of the idea of leaving town for a little while. I have to admit, at first I was surprised as I had never thought of anything like that, but it was a sensible idea, I wanted us to keep safe. Also my little sisters were terrified. Bella was staying under the table, and they both were crying and sad.

So, five hours after the earthquake, we had packed, organized someone to take care of our pets, and left, to stay with our extended family in Southland. At 2am, the next day, we arrived, having driven since 6pm the day before. On the way we visited an Aunty in Dunedin too. The next five days were honestly very strange, being hundreds of kilometres away, having a holiday, only connected to our own city by TV, text and the internet. It was almost hard to believe that it was our own city, hidden amongst the rubble.

When we got back, we wanted some way to help those who needed it, and so put on a sausage sizzle to raise money, as well as digging silt out in the hard-hit areas.

Now, a few months later, everything seems quite different, although the same in some ways. Although we are very fortunate to be reasonably unaffected, others aren't so lucky. Cantabrians are still recovering from the physical scars, emotional scars, and yes, financial scars of a disaster in our own city. Commemorating the dead, and pointing the way to an amazing future ahead, the memorial service in Hagley Park was a great way for us to all get together again. Also, I think the Japan disaster has also helped us see that although we are suffering, we can still unite to help others a long way away by land, but now not so far away in our experiences. I am looking forward to an even more beautiful city, which will do more than match the strength of its citizens.

Unexpected by Hannah Davey – age 17

I was at Burnside High School when the earthquake struck. Lunch was just coming to an end and I was heading downstairs with a friend. As we descended, the block started to shake slightly, but we carried on walking, not too bothered, thinking it was just another aftershock. But when it hadn't stopped after about 10 or 15 seconds, we paused and looked at each other.

For a split second all I wanted to do was scream, grab hold of my friend, and succumb to panic, but I managed to stay calm and we both grabbed onto the stair railings. It was nothing like the September earthquake. Instead of the building just shaking, this time it literally moved from side to side. We stood there, frozen while it was happening, the noise of screaming coming from all around.

We just stood there for a while, then commented on the Year 9s screaming downstairs. We stood for a while longer, then suddenly remembered that we'd been told that it was especially unsafe to be on stairs during an earthquake. This in mind, and voiced by both of us, we moved down to the bottom of the stairs and stood there dumbly until the earthquake had mostly subsided and the ground was only moving faintly beneath our feet. The best way I can describe the fading of the earthquake is like when you're hit with a sudden dizzy spell, and the earth doesn't feel like it's where it's supposed to be beneath your feet, and you're pretty sure you'll topple over any second because it's so unsteady. Only it's not in your head, the ground is actually moving.

Just as it was stopping our 10-minute warning bell, which sounds every lunch time, went. Most pupils treated this like the emergency bell signal, and immediately headed out onto the upper fields. As Burnside is such a large school (2 700 children) it is divided up into divisions, North, South, West and Senior, and we each have our own emergency meeting places, all in various positions along the field.

Just after I managed to find my teacher there was the first large aftershock. Immediately pupils reached out to each other in shock, some hugging each other for support. Again there were screams, mostly from the younger pupils. I was still reasonably calm at this point and looked around. As I did, I observed a large group of teachers, who had been huddled on the grass outside the classroom with radios and the like trying to figure out a plan to make sense of the chaos. They immediately moved away from the block and the large trees growing next to it, which were again swaying alarmingly.

As soon as this aftershock was over teachers began to move us further out onto the field. Up until then we had been reasonably close to both the blocks and the tall trees, and this was a worry, in case something collapsed. A lot of people were also frantically trying to contact family, especially those with family in the centre of town, as instinctively we all knew that that would be the place most hard-hit. Texts could be sent, but phoning wasn't working so a lot of people were very worried that they could not contact their families. This panic was exacerbated as people were still able to access the internet on their phones and went onto Geonet (a site where they put up information on recent earthquakes) and soon the news was flying around that it was a 6.3 on the Richter scale and only five kilometres deep, which we all knew meant it would be very bad.

Amazingly no one was hurt, surprising in a school of so many pupils, although I put this down partly to the fact that most pupils were outside because it was lunch. Had the earthquake occurred 15 or 20 minutes later, I have no doubt that I and many more would have been injured as we would all have been in class by then.

Upon arriving home I was greatly relieved to find my house in one piece, although one bookshelf had fallen over and my room was a complete mess, as things had fallen off shelves and half the water in the fish tank was gone. Once I had made sure that my fish were alright, I posted a status on Facebook saying that I was okay and had a quick look for my cat. I retired underneath the kitchen table with my laptop, a pile of DVDs, my cell phone and my pillows and a blanket.

No one died in the September earthquake, which was one of the many reasons I was much less affected by everything, including the aftershocks. However, it just made this earthquake all the more shocking, traumatising and horrific. Even though no one I knew died, or was trapped or missing, it still affected me. I could not bear to watch the news and I refused to look at pictures of the destruction. It terrified me that that it possibly could have been me, or a member of my family, or one of my friends. The aftershocks affected me a lot more than the first time and I was unashamed to admit that while I was at home I carried my teddy bear with me, clutching it for comfort whenever an aftershock hit. If one of my friends were here, or a member of my family close enough, I would cling to them instead.

On the first Wednesday night, I slept underneath the kitchen table, on edge because the aftershocks were quite close. The next morning my father said that one of the people at our church had contacted our head deacon, asking for help to clear the results of liquefaction from his house. Thankful for an opportunity to do something useful and to be around other people, I immediately asked to go with him, and spent my morning shovelling silt from his driveway and behind the house. It was a lot better than the way I spent Wednesday, huddled on the couch all day, trying to distract myself from the fear I was feeling.

After the September earthquake we slowly began to recover, putting books back on shelves, rebuilding and getting pipes reconnected. Mainly we thought it was over, that we would have minor aftershocks for the predicted six months to a year and then our lives would go back to normal. But after the February earthquake I was not entirely sure what normal was anymore, or how to go back to it. How was I supposed to go back to school and carry on my life when I was constantly afraid that there will be another quake, something that I knew was very possible?

Chapter Thirteen – People Reach out to Christchurch

In the days that followed the February earthquake, the residents of Christchurch were stunned, grief stricken and overwhelmed by the enormity of what had happened. The city was battered by frequent aftershocks and television carried breaking news as urban search and rescue teams pulled bodies from rubble. The television was our link to what was happening in the city centre and those of us lucky enough to have power, watched images of devastation, cried over the immensity of our loss and prayed for strength to get through each of those dark days. Rescue teams arrived from around the world and we watched as they cleared rubble and burrowed into collapsed buildings. The whole city mourned over the fate of Christchurch Cathedral. Situated at the heart of the CBD, it was the icon of the city and the collapse of its tower and part of the church struck deep into our hearts.

The less damaged malls were closed for two weeks and all schools were shut for at least three weeks. The sound of sirens and helicopters overhead became part of life and for some people, so did queuing for water. Many people were housed in welfare centres, unable to return to homes that had collapsed or were uninhabitable. Many had no power and no water; no way to cook, shower and wash clothes. Toilets were dug in back gardens and photos of the most creative ones were shown on television.

For the first few days, most people holed up at home. Thousands of others left Christchurch to seek refuge with family and friends. Trade Me set up a page where people travelling out of the city could offer lifts to people. I had a work trip three hours south on the Friday after the earthquake and picked up a lady who wanted to spend time with her family in Oamaru. We shared our shock and disbelief at what had happened to our city and she said she was looking forward to spending time with her mother away from the aftershocks.

While in Oamaru and Timaru, I decided to do some grocery shopping as the few stores that were open back home were empty of basics. I was dismayed to find their shelves were also empty. There was no bread, no rice, no flour. I also discovered that all petrol pumps within an hour of Christchurch had run dry.

However, there was an upside to all this. The trauma caused a new bonding between people. This had been seen after the September earthquake but as the aftershocks, lessened, people got comfortable again and started withdrawing from those around them.

When someone asked how you were after the February earthquake, it wasn't just a social nicety. It was a genuine question. Strangers chatted on street corners and acquaintances embraced each other, tears in their eyes as they asked about family members and friends. Churches filled on the first Sunday as Mayor Bob Parker encouraged people to congregate together and support each other.

The earthquake also prompted a great response from welfare organisations and many groups arrived in the city to help with the relief efforts. The Salvation Army and Red Cross were two of these. Heather Simpson of Wanaka volunteered to help through the Salvation Army and tells her story below.

Earthquake Response – Christchurch 20-25th March 2011 by Heather Simpson

After the second major quake in Christchurch, it seems likely that most of us were wondering if and how we could respond. On a personal note, my first response was to family and I had my brother and sister-in-law staying with me in Wanaka from 1st-16th March. Their situation reflected many I met later in Christchurch, that is, the need to escape the constant aftershocks and address the stress and lack of sleep. Having Rob and Margaret here was a special time. Catching up with most of my family in Christchurch later was also special, and there may yet be one or two who come this way for a break. It is tough living in the chaos and uncertainties that are in Christchurch at the moment.

When the invitation was given to join teams from around New Zealand, working under the Salvation Army umbrella in Christchurch, I was quick to respond. Needless to say this was an amazing time with some great highs, and some tough realities to absorb. My story is broken into three parts – the Salvation Army, the week's work, and my personal reflections:

The Salvation Army

It doesn't surprise me that the Salvation Army was heading up this initiative. Since the September quake they have been active in the spiritual, moral and physical support of those with major responsibilities in Christchurch, with response teams accompanying engineers, Civil Defence and the Earthquake Commission. This became more urgent after the February quake.

The Salvation Army (SA) has an international Rapid Response Team, including some Kiwis. While I was in Christchurch there were at least two from Australia on the team, and one from the US. Their expertise in organising and coordinating a response in the face of disaster was clearly evident (despite the odd hiccup), from my perspective, as a participant.

People came from all around New Zealand and Australia, the majority from SA corps, and a cross section of people from other denominations. Each team of 13 was headed up by a SA officer, and divided into six pairs, with one pair becoming the Flying Squad. The purpose of the teams was to visit house to house in designated parts of Christchurch, assess immediate and/or urgent needs, including emotional, and follow-up appropriately. Where possible, follow-up was immediate, some within a few days.

Quite apart from the 'on the ground' teams, there were other aspects of the earthquake response that made up a much larger puzzle – communications and public relations; statistics; coordination with & accessing Westpac, Caltex, PostiePlus, Countdown, chemical toilets, travel department; accommodation; transport; telephone teams; caterers; food banks ... to name a few.

The Salvation Army (as I understand it) were commissioned by the government to undertake this task, and as already mentioned there are ongoing partnerships with Christchurch quake leadership and other organisations at the coalface. Partnerships also included contacts with groups such as Red Cross, Mental Health, counselling groups, Age Concern, food banks, etc. Referrals could be passed onto these groups.

Community Help Centres had been set up around the city, and each of these centres included representatives from ACC, Housing Corp, EQC, banks, Red Cross and Salvation Army, among others.

The Salvation Army Earthquake Response group coordinated also with local SA churches, and both the Linwood and Aranui churches became centres for the reception of bulk food, its distribution to the teams, food & clothing and counselling.

I have nothing but praise for the Salvation Army. I suspect they are the only denomination that is prepared and equipped to respond rapidly to disasters and chaos. Their high profile and reputation provides automatic recognition and respect. It was a privilege to be part of such a team.

The week's work

Each day started at 7am with a cooked or cereal breakfast at Sydenham SA. At 8am we met together in the chapel for devotions after which we met as teams, and coordinated the day's activities. By 9am we were on the road to our area, with each team having a van and a car.

161

We took packed lunches with us, and were back at Sydenham by 5pm. Between 5-6pm we held a debrief, and dinner was served after that. So, it was a 12 hour day.

Our team consisted of folk from Wellington, Hamilton, Australia and Auckland and we were assigned to Burwood, Linwood and Lyttelton. I was partnered with Gareth from Wellington to be our team's flying squad. The purpose of the flying squad was to follow up immediately, or as soon as possible, any particular needs that had become obvious to the others as they visited house to house and gathered details and concerns. This meant that we spent more time with fewer people, heard in greater depth people's stories and we were able to offer some immediate help. Listening was key, and some counselling as we saw fit. Some folk needed some financial help and we were able to offer Caltex cards, cards for groceries or clothing, bucket / chemical toilets, food boxes, and in some cases, we were authorised to act like a bank and provide a debit Visa card loaded with $500. We were also able to provide contacts for counselling and other help that we felt was needed. Through the SA there was a Get Away package (up to $2500, anywhere in NZ) available for any we thought really urgently needed to get away from the city. We connected the package provider and the needy person, but ultimately we weren't party to any decisions made. Hopefully, positive!

Common phrases heard included: 'it is so good to talk to someone' (many had seen EQC, engineers, etc, but no one to really talk to); when help was offered, 'there are people much worse off than we are'; 'it's only material possessions we have lost; we have each other, that's what's important'; 'it's not the quake so much, but the aftershocks, and lack of sleep'; 'thank you, thank you,

162

thank you, the SA are such great people'; 'I used to belong to the SA'; After 4 weeks much of the infrastructure of life was getting back to a new normal. What were beginning to surface were the longer term traumas, psychological, physical, economical ... and these will need serious consideration over the next weeks. Children especially are affected, as are the elderly who were in homes. Counselling services will be overloaded, and/or not available.

Each night when I returned to my family I told them of the day's activities, and at the same time I taped the stories. Eventually I will get around to writing them all up. Here are a few brief notes about my experiences:

- The woman who lost her daughter in the CTV building; able to provide 'Take a Break', and she was looking forward to going to Auckland.
- The woman with terminal cancer, trying to cope with her 87 year old mother who had lost her home and future when Kate Sheppard Retirement home was destroyed ... a listening ear, some boundaries discussed.
- The woman stuck in panic and fear, refusing to leave home, except to get food; she had a prem baby and a 7 year old who was not happy with her mum's decision to not let her go outside ... listening, Take a Break, medical follow-up, counselling.
- The family who lost their home in the CBD, temporary housing, trying to find a new place to live, travel costs for school & work, grief in losing all possessions ... listening, petrol card.

- The man who was at breaking point; he'd lost his business premises, working from a garage, desperate to get out of town, a partner who refused to go. Really struggling emotionally ... follow-up arranged.

- The very pragmatic solo Mum, four kids including three teenage daughters, two of who had lost their jobs in the CBD. Too proud to ask for help, but overwhelmed when we able to offer financial assistance.

- The young woman taking a new grip on life after living through the quake in Lyttelton; she had accessed the least likely place in NZ to have an earthquake (Kerikeri), and was moving the day we visited. Emotional support, prayer and some tips on dealing with the future.

- The young Mum recently returned from Australia; had lost two children to illness, one wee boy just starting school; husband absconded back to Oz after the quake – she commented that she felt better in a place where everyone was experiencing pain and chaos, than in Oz where no one was experiencing her grief; emotional support and financial help.

Personal reflections

What a privilege to be a part of a response group in Christchurch. It went a long way to satisfying my heart's desire to be involved ... I would love to consider any further opportunities to help out in Christchurch.

Being a part of the Sallies was a great experience; Christ centered; known in and to the community for doing good in Christ's name; the sense of inclusion as we came from other denominations; the great organisation and rapid response in a time of dire need; the variety of services, partnerships and networks; the body working together ...

Personally, I was very grateful to God for having anticipated my health needs – being in the flying squad and with our own car meant I wasn't exacerbating the planta faciitis; I suspect I would have found the door to door too much pressure on the foot. Secondly, staying with family and not staying for tea meant that I could better control the stress on my head, keeping the concussion headaches to a minimum.

The invitation into people's stories was an amazing gift, and a sense of the Spirit leading at times to pray, or speak more directly about God's love ... these were gifts beyond imagining.

Because we were in and out of each area on a daily basis this meant we have no control on any follow-up ... people we have connected for a holiday, or counselling, or further help via the Salvation Army telephone service. It's not always easy to let go of a story mid-way, with the likelihood that we will never know how things evolved. Trusting the Sallies with the next steps is key for me at this stage!

It's really great that the Salvation Army are set up and ready to go in such situations. It is also great that they invite others to participate, as well as the incredible respect and open doors the Sallies have. People know without clarification what the SA stands for – they are Christians and they help. They have done an amazing job in Christchurch and have the infrastructure to implement a long term, coordinated response in times of disaster.

Chapter Fourteen - Financial Support for Christchurch

New Zealand people are generous givers. Thousands of people donate to charity on a regular basis and many more have sponsor children in poorer nations. Over the course of the Christchurch earthquakes, the country dug deep and millions of dollars were given to various funds and charities working in the city. For the people in Christchurch it was strange to be on the receiving end. Things like this weren't supposed to happen to us. Our city was supposed to be safe. The images on television looked like a disaster zone in a poor third world country, not our home.

The damage in Christchurch is estimated in tens of billions of dollars and each large aftershock adds to the bill. The Earthquake has listed all of the large earthquakes and aftershocks as separate events for insurance purposes.

While there is a certain amount of provision for rebuilding the shattered infrastructure and broken buildings, there were many cases of people falling through the cracks and needing financial support to tide them through difficult patches. Some had expenses related to moving home while others had to face costs associated with injury or emergency repairs. The Red Cross was one group who did a fantastic job with supporting individuals. Over the months they made a number of grants available to people who had been without power and water, to those who had lost homes and had to relocate and to those who faced high power bills in the winter that followed the earthquakes.

I travel extensively for work purposes and in the weeks after each of the big earthquakes, my heart was touched as I visited destinations that included Auckland, Wellington, Napier, Invercargill, Queenstown, Dunedin, Oamaru, Timaru, Ashburton and numerous tiny towns. Billboards proclaimed, 'Christchurch we Love You', and stores had large signs up asking people to donate to Christchurch. Staff members in stores asked me to buy charity bags for $2 with funds going to Christchurch. Other stores had collection boxes stuffed with cash and a place to drop in donations of canned food and blankets. The level of support was overwhelming.

A few days after the February earthquake I flew into Auckland and saw tables set up to welcome people fleeing from Christchurch. Counselling and support were available and representatives from various embassies were there to help stranded tourists. Announcements encouraged anyone arriving from Christchurch to go and have a chat as people were waiting to help them.

Soon after the September earthquake, people started using their creativity to raise funds for Christchurch. Ideas included silver, broken-house charms for bracelets, red cross pendants, children's books, photo mounts, coffee tables, T-shirts and busking. A couple of weeks after the first earthquake, I was in Cathedral Square and saw a couple of young boys entertaining passers-by. One was singing while the other played a guitar. I went closer and saw a sign propped up next to a collection bucket. They had official busker's permits from the Christchurch City Council and a sign up that announced that all proceeds that day would be given to the Mayoral Earthquake Fund.

I'm a keen photographer and my collection of earthquake photos dates back to early on the 4th September. In October 2010 I decided to take the best shots and compile them into a professionally printed photo book to preserve memories for family in years to come. I did an internet search and found that Photobook.co.nz offered a good price and were based in Christchurch. Using their template I set up a book and ordered two copies: one for myself and one for a friend. The quality was excellent and when I showed friends, a number of them expressed interest in buying a copy. That was the birth of my Trade Me business. From the outset, I determined that all profits would go to the Red Cross earthquake appeal and every few weeks I paid money over to them. I ended up using three different printers and expanded the range to include postcards, fridge magnets, giant photo canvases, T-shirts, mugs, notebooks, calendars, and a range of photo books. All of these bore images of earthquake damage – and to many I added a Bible verse or an expression of hope.

Christchurch Earthquake 2010

September 4th 2010, 4:35 am
Photography by Debbie Roome

Like anything in life, there were moments when I wondered why I was doing it. Nearly every morning I packed orders and became an expert on the postal system in New Zealand. I stocked up on courier bags, fast post stickers and prepaid envelopes. I learnt how much each item cost to post and the best way to package it. While most Trade Me customers loved my stuff, there were a couple who returned items. One person even reported me to the Red Cross thinking I was pocketing the money and not passing on the proceeds. Fortunately the Red Cross had records of all the credit card payments I'd made and wrote to this person telling them that I was definitely passing the funds on to them. Over the months, I sent hundreds of orders to destinations around New Zealand and was awarded Top Seller status on Trade Me. Many purchases came with a personal message, wishing us well in Christchurch and telling us that they were thinking of us. Then there were the steady stream of Christchurch locals who came to my home to pick up their orders.

Most of them lingered for a while and told me why they had bought the items. Many were sending books to relatives overseas while others bought things that had personal meaning. I think of the man whose wife was next to the Provincial Chambers when the February earthquake struck. She was terribly traumatised and wanted to leave Christchurch. Her husband bought a giant canvas print of the damaged Provincial buildings as well as a mug with the same picture on. He hoped they would be part of her healing as well as a memory to look back on.

I think also of the lady who sat with me and told of shovelling silt and helping in welfare centres. Of how she wanted to make a difference in any way she could. A customer from Methven requested photo prints of all my business-card size fridge magnets. She wanted them for memories but couldn't bear to see them on her fridge every day. A number of people overpaid me, saying the extra was to go to the Red Cross. All of them had a story and all expressed pain over what had happened to our city.

Although I set up the Trade Me business purely to help the Red Cross, it turned out to have a personal benefit to me. A number of book sellers/library suppliers around New Zealand heard about my photo books and asked if they could list them. As a result, I sold dozens of copies through them and my books are now available in many New Zealand libraries including Auckland, Wellington and Christchurch.

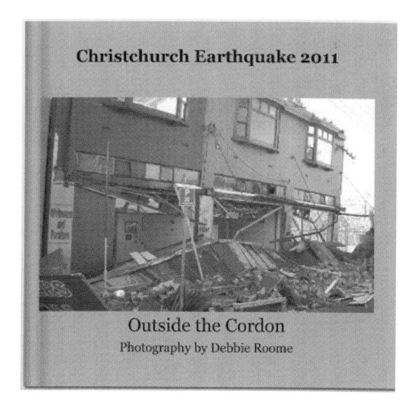

A Helping Hand from Afar by Diane Jones

Those of us living in Vancouver, BC, Canada, have a double kinship with Christchurch, New Zealand. First, our two countries are members of the family known as the Commonwealth of Nations. As such, we share not only a common language, but very similar histories and cultures.

Second, like New Zealand, the west coast of British Columbia is situated on an earthquake fault. In Vancouver, we are well aware that we will one day be hit by the "big one." We have small, but usually imperceptible earthquakes almost daily, but the series of quakes and aftershocks in New Zealand have jolted us in a different way. We are now more aware that what happened in Christchurch can and probably will happen to Vancouver.

Sandwiched between the disasters that hit Haiti (January 12, 2010) and Japan (March 11, 2011), the devastation experienced by Christchurch on February 22, 2011 seems to have been forgotten by the world media. Not so in this city. The Anglican cathedral in Vancouver is called Christ Church Cathedral. On hearing of the New Zealand tragedy, especially of the extensive damage done to New Zealand's Christchurch Cathedral, Dean Peter Elliott of Vancouver sent a message to the deans of all other North American cathedrals that share the name. He invited them to commit to daily prayer support in addition to financial support as each is able.

So, while we support our New Zealand family in these ways, we wait and watch and learn, knowing that one day it will be our turn.

Chapter Fifteen – Not Again – June 13th 2011

The 13th June started like any other day for me. I travel frequently and on that morning, I was booked to fly to Palmerston North in the North Island of New Zealand. It was a short trip and my flight home was due to depart at 1pm. I got my work done in the central city, browsed around one of the malls, bought a few items and treated myself to butter chicken for lunch. I was quite content as I boarded the aircraft to fly home.

We took off on schedule and had been in the air for a few minutes when the pilot made an announcement. "I've just been informed that Christchurch has had another large aftershock. We're cleared to continue the flight but the navigational equipment at the airport will have to be checked before we can land."

My heart froze. *How big was the aftershock? Is my family safe? Will we be allowed to land?* Ever since the September earthquake, I'd suffered from mild anxiety when flying out of Christchurch. It was always at the back of my mind that something major might happen to close the airport and separate me from my family. I spent a restless half hour until the pilot told us we were clear to land and the aftershock had been a 5.3.

Our approach took us past the CBD of Christchurch and as I was on the right side of the plane to see the view, I zoomed in and took several shots that included Christchurch Cathedral. I remembered the dust cloud that had enveloped the city after the February earthquake and thought *I'm glad that's not likely to happen again.* We circled around to the airport and landed at exactly 2:20pm. I switched my cell phone on as we were taxiing in and dialled Kevin's number as he was going to pick me up and drop me at home. It was inaccessible. I tried twice more and then put my phone away as we pulled up by the terminal building. As I disembarked, I noticed that a fire engine had pulled up next to us and a bunch of guys jumped out in hi-visibility vests. I instinctively turned to look at the aircraft to see if it had caught fire.

It was only as I entered the terminal building that I realized what was going on. Staff were running around shouting and passengers surged towards the exits. "Get out! We're evacuating! Get out now!" I followed the crush of people, slowly putting the pieces together. *There must have been a second big aftershock. Where is Kevin? Where are the children? Are they safe?* Outside the airport, people tried frantically to call and text while security ensured no one entered the terminal buildings or multi-level car park.

I had never felt so alone. My hands trembled as I dialled one family member after another only to hear engaged signals. The road to the airport was blocked off and no one was being allowed in so I started walking home. There were at least a dozen other people on the road and their faces reflected mine. Despair, shock, horror, uncertainty. I still had no idea how big the earthquake had been, if it had caused further damage and what had happened to the city and surrounds.

I finally got hold of my youngest son, Daniel, and asked him to pick me up at the traffic circle near the airport. He filled me in and told me there had been another major aftershock that initially registered as a 6.0.

Once home, I turned the TV on and live broadcasts showed liquefaction had again caused flooding and massive deposits of silt, rocks had tumbled from cliffs and more buildings had collapsed. Like the majority of Christchurch, I was gutted. *Not another one. How could this happen again? We had just started making progress towards recovery.* The two big shakes were later upgraded to a 5.7 and a 6.3.

As mentioned earlier, my son, Tim's 21st celebration was overshadowed by the 22nd February earthquake. Unbelievably, Kevin's birthday coincided with the 13th June earthquake. I had a sense of déjà vu as I scratched through the grocery cupboard and looked for ingredients to cook him a birthday dinner. All the malls and shops were closed again and but we managed to find a dairy that was open. Instead of ice cream and fruit for dessert that night, we made do with sweet Chinese tarts! For me, that day was one of the lowest points since the September earthquake. I wondered what our futures in Christchurch looked like and how much longer the ground would heave and lift beneath us.

I went out the next morning, camera in hand, and drove through various parts of the city. Roads were buckled and flooded and thick layers of silt smothered pavements and gardens. People had marked massive sink holes by placing large wheelie bins inside them. As I drove past Redcliffs, I saw part of a home had plummeted to sea level where the edge of the cliffs had fallen away. A number of other houses teetered on the precipice, walls missing, contents exposed for the world to see.

I ended my journey in Sumner where the people were without power and water. Emergency workers were handing out bottled water and a large tanker supplied water for washing and other basic needs. There was a queue of people waiting with containers and their expressions said it all. Brokenness, disbelief and sorrow ... and yet in the midst of it all, some still smiled and laughed with each other. An elderly man walked over to me. "How're you doing? Are you alright? Is your family okay?" The concern of a complete stranger lifted my spirits. I'd made it through the September and February earthquakes and aftermath. I would get through this one as well.

When we Came to the Conference by Ruth Linton

"Aren't you afraid of going to Christchurch with all those earthquakes?" our cleaner asked when she heard the Christian Camping New Zealand Conference was to be held at Living Springs Camp on the Lyttelton side of the Port Hills. "Isn't there a safer place you could go?"

My husband and I were keen to support our South Island camping 'family' but were we afraid to go? I pondered the question often and concluded I was as apprehensive about the flight down (I love flying but didn't know how to check in luggage and get all the necessary

181

pre-flight checks done) as I was about the earthquakes. I'd never experienced one before so how could I be scared of something I had no comprehension of?

"Lord, I refuse to be afraid of something I know nothing about," I prayed many times in the days before our departure.

We flew from Auckland to Christchurch early on the morning of Monday June 13th.Our drive from Christchurch Airport, through the city and over to the camp was interesting and unnecessarily long. A friend had given us directions using roads she knew were open, but we still lost our way several times. Concentrating on reading street names and stopping often to consult our map meant we didn't see any of the earthquake damage we had heard so much about.

"I'm glad we don't have to go through the Lyttelton Tunnel," I said as we wound over Dyers Pass. "I loathe going underground and what would happen if there was an earthquake while we were in it?"

"Wow! What a view." My husband enthused as we looked out over the Lyttelton Harbour before winding down to the Governors Bay-Teddington Road below.

Living Springs Camp is set in farm land with patches of bush, fascinating outcrops of volcanic rock and more stunning views of the harbour. It seemed remote from Christchurch and very safe and peaceful. We were glad our conference was being held there.

The morning sessions passed as scheduled, followed by a delicious lunch served in a high-ceilinged dining room warmed with a lovely open fire. We chatted to folks from Christian camps throughout New Zealand. In fact the conference was smaller than usual as many had chosen not to come because of possible earthquakes and aftershocks, and the ash cloud from the Chilean volcano had caused other people's flights to be cancelled.

We were stunned by the suddenness of the first quake. Conversation stopped abruptly. Should we run? I gazed nervously upward to be sure I wasn't under a heavy beam. We started to push out our chairs ready to bolt.

"Stay where you are," the camp hostess called. "You're safe where you are." We were amazed at the staff's apparent confidence. "It's probably about a 5.3 magnitude and we've had those before without any damage."

We were not totally convinced but conversation slowly resumed.

We had been issued a bag containing emergency supplies—torch, ponchos, snacks and the like—and were now encouraged to keep them handy. We were also reminded of the evacuation point near the flag pole. My husband and I had a bedroom downstairs so I hoped the building wouldn't collapse on our head. I counted the steps—thirteen down to the bedroom and another four down to the toilets and showers—to enable me to find my way in the dark if need be. *How,* I wondered, *would you cope if an earthquake struck while you were in the shower or occupied in the toilet?*

We settled into our first afternoon session and I was rather distracted by the fabulous view from the Harbour View Lounge we were seated in. I suppose, if we had been thinking about it, we may have noticed the approaching rumble, but we didn't. Suddenly the room shook with a violent force. We stood as one and made for the door.

Shall I stand under the door frame? I paused for a fraction of a second.

"Keep walking," a man hissed. I did.

The flag pole. Go to the flag pole. Almost without conscious approval my feet took me there without even grabbing my emergency bag. We knew it must have been a big quake as the staff had also evacuated.

The ground continued to rumble for some time. We talked excitedly but had no idea what we should do. Parents worried about the children involved in the youth programme. In less than a minute they came marching into view and were greeted with generous hugs of relief. Seaward we could see clouds of dust rising off the harbour heads and the end of Quail Island where cliffs had tumbled.

While the staff checked the buildings we continued to talk. Several people from Christchurch had come to take workshops at the conference so we included them in our nervous chatter:

"Was your home badly affected in September or February?"

"What do you do with all the silt and sand?"

"I tried it on the garden," one said, "but it was useless. Nothing grew."

It took several minutes for the camp staff to organise us into groups to check that everyone was safe. We were still talking as if to prove we were not afraid so every instruction needed to be repeated several times.

"Are you worried about your husband" someone asked. He was with a small group of men looking at the Camp's water and sewage systems.

"No," I replied. "I know where they went and I can see the workshop from here. Nothing untoward seems to be happening there." Sure enough, about ten minutes later the group arrived back quite unscathed. The leader,

184

however, stayed behind to repair a pipe line that had ruptured in the quake.

The conversations continued for over an hour. Talking seemed to distract us and we talked unnaturally loudly. Finally, just as the evening chill set in, we were able to return inside. The power was out but the camp was undamaged. Fortunately, the camp had its own water supply and sewage system which would operate satisfactorily for several hours. The kitchen staff turned on the generator and prepared a sumptuous dinner. Meanwhile we attended the final workshop of the day fighting with the fading light. I made sure I was near a door and checked which way to evacuate should there be another quake.

Later we ate our delicious evening meal by candle light. The staff used the generator to power a large television screen so we could see the news of the day. We almost felt proud; we had survived a major earthquake. We felt like heroes!

The power was still not on after our evening church service so we went to bed by torchlight. Before retiring we checked our emergency bags and made sure we could grab them easily in the dark. I thought it was a good idea to put a complete change of warm clothes in the boot of our rental car. The idea of standing outside in the dark, in pyjamas was not appealing.

I don't think any of us slept more than a quarter of an hour at a time all through the night. I know I didn't! During the night the power returned. Through the wall I could hear what I assumed was the water cylinder switching on and off. Every half hour or so it would rumble for a minute. Instantly, I'd be wide awake.

Is that another quake? I thought each time.

It was 4.20 am when the next big aftershock (4.7) hit. Instantly we were wide awake, sitting bolt upright on the edge of the bed with one hand clutching our emergency bags.

Shall we evacuate? It's awfully dark still. Thank God, the quake passed quickly and we cuddled back in bed pretending to sleep.

As the light gradually crept into the bedroom I thought of the verse from the Bible: 'Weeping may endure for the night but joy comes in the morning.'

I even risked a quick shower, having first placed my emergency bag right next to the door in case it was needed. I was full of joy. I had survived an earthquake. Over breakfast we discovered the previous day's quakes had been upgraded to 5.7 and 6.3, centred to the right of Lyttelton, and that much more damage had occurred.

"Lord, have mercy on the people of Christchurch," I prayed often.

Over the following week we experienced more smaller aftershocks and quickly learned to assess their intensity.

"That's a four point something," or "That's probably a five," we'd say. The tiny quakes hardly deserved a mention! Gradually, too, we learned to sleep through the little ones. We almost felt invincible, I think, since no one had been hurt or killed.

During the next three or four days we had the chance to tour some of the city by bus and, later, a friend took us around the CBD. We saw places where rocks had literally flown out of hillsides and landed on houses. We saw many older, traditional churches in ruins; we saw soldiers guarding cordoned areas against looters; we saw graffitied port-a-loos. Human nature is still corrupt! I thought the ruins would make me cry as had some of the television news reports had, but it was easy to slip into the tourist mode and click, click, click with the camera.

In contrast to the broken churches, we visited two who have had a tremendous impact in the city, one feeding ten thousand people after the February quake and another providing a variety of initiatives for on-going assistance in the town, especially among students. We met a principal whose school had been relocated three times and was now in restrictive premises. It was an honour to donate towards sports gear and books for the students. Yes, the positive side of human nature was often seen too.

We visited friends, admired their courage as they faced an uncertain future and sensed their frustration at the lack of progress. But, how can one progress when the quakes keep shaking? We sat in one friend's lounge and watched the lights shake as a 4.5 and a 3.9 rattled through, shaking more plaster dust over the furniture which had been cleaned and vacuumed only minutes before. Our friend hadn't bothered to clear up items tossed on the floor the previous day. The doors didn't shut, the mantle-piece had fallen, the ceiling and walls were covered with cracks and her file of broken items, meticulously photographed and prepared for valuation, was already more than six centimetres deep.

How can you face that day after day? I wondered.

"Thank you for coming," she said. "I've been feeling really down. How special it was to have someone pray for me in my own home!"

At midday on Saturday we returned our rental car and arrived at the airport ready to fly home. How blessed we felt. The ash cloud from the Chilean volcano had moved so we were able to fly as planned. There'd been no more major earthquakes so the airport was open.

"It'll be nice to be home, away from the continual anxious anticipation of earthquakes," my husband commented, and I agreed.

We sank into our seats in the plane. This time we were right above the wings so our view was restricted but it didn't matter. We were going home! As we taxied down the runway and lifted off I started to cry. Yes, we'd experienced some shattering events. We had seen unbelievable sights and we'd felt the pain of a city eager to rebuild but stymied on every side. It was overwhelming! Frustrating! But, I wouldn't have missed the experience for anything.

In God's time, I'll be back.

Pain by Ruth Linton

Pain…

The emotional terror,

The physical rock and roll,

The earthquake

Upending our world

Crumbling our proud history

And compressing away the life

Of friends caught in the debris

Pain …

The realisation

Nothing will ever be the same again

The landmarks we trusted

Trashed or, at best, askew.

The people we loved

Have aged, moved out, or passed away.

Pain …

The daily routine

Of boiled water and port-a-loos

Novel at first but with no end in sight

Deadens hope, manic rage incites.

Nine months have shaken past,

No insurance pay-out has eventuated.

Surely Council, Government,

Someone must be to blame?

Can't anyone do better than this?

Pain …

The numbing cold blast

Of winter whirling down our street,

It's hard to keep warm when the house is still cracked!

Yes, the power is on and the telephone rings

But the roof still leaks and the wall still leans

And bureaucracy seems

To move faster in reverse.

Pain …

Being forced to traverse

Roads repeatedly patched

Buildings condemned daily—beyond repair

At first there was hope, but now I'm resigned:

The final acknowledgement numbs my mind:

My home can't be sold or given away!

I have to stay here and wait …and wait …and pray

For some means to rebuild—does anyone care?

The aftershocks keep rumbling

And the dash to the port-a-loo is colder each day!

Chapter Sixteen –Social Networking in 2011and Earthquakes in 1929

Social networking and the internet have played an enormous role in the Christchurch earthquakes. News of the 7.1 shake was relayed on Twitter within a couple of minutes of it happening and texts, tweets and status updates on Facebook have continued ever since. I picked up my laptop to go onto Facebook a few minutes after the September earthquake but we lost power to our home before I managed to get online. When a major disaster such as an earthquake strikes, most people's initial reaction is 'Where is my family? Is everyone safe?' After the 7.1 and both 6.3 shakes, the cell phone network in Christchurch was stretched to capacity and in many cases, failed. The phone companies appealed to the public to text rather than call but even so, messages and calls were backed up and communication spotty. I was in a public area after the two 6.3 quakes and as soon as we were out in the open, people pulled out their phones.

The internet and technology have transformed the face of natural disasters such as those that Christchurch has lived through. People snapped pictures on cell phones while fleeing town on the 22nd February. Others captured video footage and recorded the sounds and images of terror and panic. These photos and clips made their way on to YouTube, Facebook and other social networking sites as well as being run on television. It was as though everyone had become a journalist, spreading the news to family and friends – especially those who did not live in Christchurch.

A couple of other sites became popular with the people in Canterbury and even further afield. The first one was Geonet.co.nz which belongs to GNS Science. This has a whole section on earthquakes including pages that show the depth and location of the last 30 earthquakes in New Zealand, a monthly forecast of expected aftershocks in Canterbury and scientific reports and data on the Christchurch earthquakes. Canterbury Quake Live was another site that became a lifeline to many. When large aftershocks awoke the city in the wee hours of the morning, thousands of people would boot up their computers, log in and wait to see how big the shake had been. This website had a number of extra features such as a link to Google maps pinpointing where the shake occurred. It also gave the distance from the epicentre to Cathedral Square and you could put in your own address to see how far it was from your home. Another useful feature was a page with graphs of all the aftershocks and a list of the top

25 shakes plus details about their strength and location. Canterbury Quake Live was linked to a Facebook page and after each large aftershock, dozens of people would interact online while waiting for the size of the tremor to be uploaded. It was interesting reading as people described how they felt the shock and what area they lived in. Any shocks over 5.0 in magnitude seemed to travel long distances and comments would surface from Ashburton, Timaru, Dunedin and even further afield.

I remember thinking during one stressful day how fortunate we were to have cell phones and technology available; that these linked us to people around Christchurch and beyond; and how a perfect stranger could offer encouragement to someone through Facebook. That led me to thinking about earthquakes in the earlier days of New Zealand's history. I remembered that I had typed out, edited and published the life story of a man who lived through the 7.8 magnitude 1929 Murchison earthquake. At the time I had thought it sounded like a nasty experience but couldn't fully comprehend what he was talking about. A few weeks after the September earthquake, I hauled his manuscript out and read it with new eyes. Suddenly it made sense. I could picture what he was saying. I could understand the emotion and feel the fear. I could see the earth split and lifted and the hills torn apart. I also realised what an incredible gift we have with modern communications. Back in 1929 news travelled slowly and there was little contact with people in the earthquake zone. Jenny McLellan has kindly given me permission to reproduce the chapter her father wrote about the Murchison earthquake.

An Eye Witness Account of the 1929 Murchison Earthquake by Robert Percy Hughes – 1899 to 1986

Once again fancy-free and seeking work, another chap and I headed off over the Takaka Hill where our destination was the Tarakohe Cement Works. It was being enlarged and a quarter million pounds was being invested in new machinery from Sweden, along with Swedish engineers to assemble it. I signed on as a fitter's labourer. With the machinery arriving very slowly, we had a lot of spare time and I managed to get in some acts of high-class mischief until I realised Takaka was populated by a lot of folk from other areas who came there as specialised workers and my pranks could not be tolerated. Seeing the writing on the wall, I became the model decent boy.

We were not there long when that mighty upheaval struck the region and along with Murchison there was death. The engineer in control of the engine room was killed by a mighty rock that fell from the hill alongside the works. Also, it was so large it smashed the entrance to a passage used by staff going and coming from the engine room. The works employed a very large force and when the roll call was called to see if all workers were accounted for, he was the only name not answered for. A search was requested and the engine room was first on the agenda. The only way in was a small hole high up in the wall on the seaward side, which needed a long ladder. Being midget-sized, I and another chap around my build were chosen. We got in and searched to no avail as there was no sign of him. Finally, we had a closer look in the passage where the rock had smashed the entrance. It had forced the outside corrugated iron wall in against the other wall, squashing the poor chap's head in and in so doing, he was lifted about

196

a foot off the ground. He was really concealed and only by very close searching, did the chap with me, notice a part of one booted-foot revealed. We made known we had located him, and with the use of crowbars, we soon had a hole in the wall and the management had him released. Death must have been very quick as there were many tons of rock that took his life.

We were a very close knit band of workers and shared the trials and tribulations of one another. That episode was a tragic tragedy, more so in the fact that he should never have been killed as when the quake first hit, he came outside to investigate and was seen by other workers. Realising it was an earth movement of considerable force, he threw all switches to safeguard the many workers from any danger as power lines carrying electric current to operate the many phases necessary could break and perhaps workers might come into contact with them. We surmise he was returning to the outside when a rock fell on him just a few feet from safety. On inspection of the fuse box, it was found all power had been disconnected. To all of us there, it was a very sobering thought as we realised he had sacrificed his life for his workmates. Without a doubt the accident rate would, I'm sure, have been greater and perhaps more serious. To me, as I record these happenings, I feel mighty proud that I knew and shared experiences with some very worthwhile folk and it really erased the hurt, or better still, as some things could never be wiped from memory. We knew there were genuine friends we could turn to who would help us.

As I cast my mind back to that sad day in June 1929, as the earth bucked and heaved killing one of our workmates, I feel I would like to quote a few words from the Scriptures which say:

Greater love hath no man than he who layeth down his own life for his brother.

I'm fully convinced there is a message to all in the everyday happenings, as I recall many fine folk, now departed, whose memory lingers down through the years. It is my ambition that when my time arrives to depart, I will do so willingly, and leave the world a little the better for having been in it. I will really feel I have achieved something. Also, along with this quotation:

Who loves his work and knows how to spare,
May live and flourish anywhere.

Many of us love our work, but how many really know how to spare? I am only 13 months off my eightieth birthday and would not qualify. This is a sobering thought and one which needs careful thought. Perhaps few might qualify more than another, but I'm sure by trying we will be aware and with willingness in trying, will certainly be on the road where our light might brighten the way for others.

After the earth movement at Tarakohe, we were laid off for a week to allow the management time to assess all damage. All sorts of rumours were coming in regarding the damage done to Murchison, such as hills being torn asunder and people killed. A state of emergency had been called and all the inhabitants were transferred to Nelson. I could see no sense in hanging around Tarakohe so high-tailed it to be with my Murchison friends. It was a sad story told by many who fled as the hills tried to stand on end, leaving housework and all chores undone. Most farmers opened all farm gates to allow stock to graze at

198

will and pigs, fowls and dogs also had free run.

Shortly after my arrival, two farmers applied for a pass to return as they feared for the survival of some stock which were in a small paddock. Not knowing the length of time ere returning, they wanted to go there and give more grazing. I decided I too wanted to go and asked their permission. I knew the answer as soon as it left my lips. Avery decided no. I made my way inside the office where they had procured their pass, and said I too wanted a pass to go. The chap asked my name and I said I was the son of the one who had a pass to return and felt I could be a help in some small way. Lo and behold, I got a pass under another name. Gee, that was a lively few minutes. Anyway, everyone thought no harm would come if I too was included.

We caught the Nelson to Glenhope railway, arriving around midnight. Glenhope was the rail end which meant we had 28 miles of foot slogging. What a journey that 28 miles in the dark and rain proved to be. Some sections of the road we journeyed over were a moving quagmire. Rocks, trees, mud and slush. Just imagine us as we negotiated the many such places along the way. Finally, we made it to our destination in the Matiri Valley and enjoyed a hot drink and some sandwiches from bread we carried from Nelson as we knew eats would not be available to us. Between the three of us we carried a light swag with the bare needs: tea, sugar, biscuits, jam and preserves were intact in the home we put up in. Really, the pantry unlike other homes was spared. Apart from a fallen chimney which had left a gaping hole in the roof as it landed in the sitting room, the damage overall was nominal. The next day we made ourselves comfortable and attended to the stock.

199

Gradually we investigated the other homes and in some we had a herculean task of cleaning jams and pickles, intermixed with glass, off the floors as the pantries had spilled their shelves. What a heart-break. One home had a piano and apparently it was left with the cover up. Fowls had been roosting on the piano and their droppings were all over the keys. All this was cleaned up, along with floors, using oceans of boiling water that we boiled up in the coppers which the homes were equipped with. The woman was never told what a mess her piano had been subjected to. What with fowls living in the houses, dogs, cats and even pigs found their way in as holes had been smashed with falling chimneys. Food had been hastily left as the folk decamped, never expecting in lots of cases, to return. No doubt the pigs smelt food and invaded the premises. We had quite a job, and seeing we had decreed we were not returning, did our best to make the places habitable should folk return. Really, we must have alarmed those in Nelson who knew we were there and had not returned, but no way was I going to do a repeat over that 28 miles of slushy mud, uprooted trees and mighty rocks. No way, even though I was a tiger for punishment. I decided I was staying and would sleep with one eye open as the quakes continued to shake. They kept it up for three weeks with an occasional heavy jolt and incessant rain, plus the noise as slips cascaded down the gullies. I can assure all and sundry I was scared stiff and never want a repetition of those 1929 days.

We had been back around three weeks when out of the blue, the husband of the woman who owned the previously mentioned piano, stumbled through the doorway – and what a mess. We cleaned him up and got a warm drink into him and listened to his tale of woe as he

200

fought the mud and slime, homeward bound to the Matiri, mainly to see if we were alright. I listened to him and every so often I would interrupt, telling him how brave he was in negotiating the mighty slips as we only had one or two minor ones to contend with. Talk about being a stirrer. I know without being told that I am the *King of Stirrers*. The other two chaps put up with my stirring for a time till one finally beckoned me outside. Waving his arms and nearly busting his gut string, he told me in no uncertain tones to shut up or else. Believe me, he did mean it. As the days passed, more male folk returned and ere long, all families were reunited with everyone joining in to help readjust.

But some things could never be put right and as I look back the fifty years and three, I can still see the scarred hills of Murchison. A reminder of the tragedy that struck on that June morning, leaving a trail of death and destruction as that small band of hard-working people, seeking to making a living so far away from the lights of the bright cities, were for their safety evacuated to Nelson. In leaving, they knew some were left behind buried under tons of rubble and rock.

The coming of the mighty 1929 earthquake changed the face of the Lyell along with the districts. Unfortunately these were in line with the fault line which is in evidence as you travel down the Buller. The scarred hills are devoid of bush which slipped off the hills as they were tossed and torn asunder at the height of the quake. These can still be seen with a barren bare-looking rock face devoid of any growth along with the roadway which was thrust 14 to 15 feet up above the original level. As I travel over the familiar route once used by me as a drover and which I now travel by motor car to visit my family in

Westport, I can say the years have brought many changes plus many heartaches.

Chapter Seventeen – Special Events Following the Christchurch Earthquakes

The people of Christchurch and Canterbury gathered together a number of times over the year following the September earthquake. The events laid on were varied but all acknowledged the effects the earthquakes had on the people. There is something healing in being with a group of others; in sharing our pain and loss as a community with people who understand.

Breakfast for Canterbury

This was the first of the large events and was held in Cathedral Square on the 24th September 2010. It took the form of a three-hour live screening by TVNZ and was described as a celebration of the region's resilience. The show was hosted by the TVNZ Breakfast team of Corin Dann, Paul Henry, PippaWetzell and Tamati Coffey. These four did a superb job of entertaining the crowd, and their guests included Christchurch Mayor Bob Parker and New Zealand Prime Minister John Key.

I arrived there just after 6am and the city looked beautiful. There was little damage in the Square at that time and the rising sun reflected off buildings in panels of pink, peach and gold. A large screen next to Christchurch Cathedral displayed news interviews and footage of the devastation caused by the earthquake, and the crowd of several thousand was treated to a free breakfast including sausage and bacon on bread, hot drinks, boxes of juice and ice creams.

Several Kiwi bands were flown in by Air New Zealand and entertained the crowds with lively music. This included songs written especially about the earthquake and Christchurch was urged to keep strong.

Throughout the breakfast, well-known figures autographed papers and photos and exchanged comments with hundreds of fans. At one stage, John Key came out of the secured area for a photo with a military group. Seeing my chance, I approached him as he walked back to the fenced enclosure. "Would you mind if I had a photo taken with you?"

He agreed with a smile and put his arm around my shoulders as I handed my camera to the nearest soldier. "I hope he doesn't do a runner with that," he joked.

The picture came out well and was the highlight of the morning for me. It was a time of hope, expectation, and appreciation of the support shown by the rest of the country. The food was greatly enjoyed and there was a genuine sense of celebration amongst the people. This was not to say the seriousness of the occasion was forgotten.

New Year in Cathedral Square

Each year, Christchurch holds a New Year event in Cathedral Square. Typically this involves a band, entertainment and a countdown of the old year followed by a firework display. The 2010 celebration was threatened by a swarm of aftershocks that caused chaos on Boxing Day. In the space of 24 hours, the city was shaken 26 times with the strongest shock being a 4.9. The epicentre of this shake was beneath the CBD and caused masonry falls and further damage to a number of buildings.

I went into town to see what had happened and found some roads closed off and collapsed awnings and piles of bricks and rubble. X Base Backpackers in Cathedral Square suffered cracking and the building was evacuated. Shocked guests sat in the Square with their bags, waiting to hear what arrangements had been made for them. The Boxing Day sales had been in full swing but shattered windows and broken stock forced stores to close.

On the morning of the 31st December, The Press reported that the New Year's Eve celebration would continue as planned in Cathedral Square. However, the public were urged to remain calm in the event of any further aftershocks. An evacuation plan was in place and people were told that if there was an emergency, they should stay calm, not panic and move quietly back to their cars and go home.

Approximately 15,000 people supported the celebration and shortly before midnight, the crowd was praised for their resilience and encouraged to look to 2011 with expectation. A traumatic 2010 came to an end as the people cheered and whistled the New Year in. Fireworks were launched from the roof of the nearby Millenium Hotel and the bells of Christchurch Cathedral rang out announcing 2011. I, along with the crowd, had no idea what the New Year was to bring us.

The Memorial Service on the 18th March

The Memorial Service on the 18th March was a chance for Christchurch to grieve together and mourn the loss of life as well as the devastation of the city. A crowd of approximately 100,000 people gathered in Hagley Park, arriving by car, bus, bicycle, and on foot. Many brought food baskets, blankets and refreshments with them. As I followed the masses streaming towards the stage area, I noticed trees decorated with broad red and black ribbons – the colours of Canterbury.

At 12:15pm, preceding the official start time of 12:30pm, Christchurch Mayor Bob Parker stood and introduced a 14-minute video that showed the earthquake damage to the centre of the city. The vast majority of Christchurch people had only seen the devastation on their television screens as the CBD was cordoned off shortly after the quake. Emergency workers and Civil Defence were the only ones allowed into the area. I fell silent with the crowd as we saw flattened buildings, crushed vehicles and streets that were no longer recognizable as home.

A number of inspiring speeches were made by dignitaries including Prince William, Prime Minister John Key, Bob Parker, and the Right Reverend Victoria Matthews. The Very Reverend Peter Beck of Christchurch Cathedral introduced the two minute silence at 12:51 pm to remember those who died at that time on the 22nd February. After a number of hymns and prayers, the service ended with the New Zealand anthem.

Although subdued, the mood of the crowd was one of hope
for the future and an acceptance of what has happened.
After the official end of the service, thousands flocked to
the front to shake hands with Prince William, John Key
and others. I joined this group and got some good photos
as well as shook hands with the Prime Minister.

For me, the Memorial Service was a turning point,
a time where I joined with those who shared my pain and
sorrow. Together we sang and prayed and processed our
loss. It was a step towards recovery.

About the Author

Debbie Roome was born and raised in Zimbabwe and later spent fifteen years in South Africa. In 2006 she moved to New Zealand with her husband and five children. Writing has been her passion since the age of six and she loves to write stories that touch people's lives and turn them towards God. Her major writing achievements include the trophy for Runner-up to the Writer of the Year, South Africa,2004; placing second out of 7000 in the FaithWriters.com "Best of the Best" contest for 2007; and receiving the trophy from the South African Writers' Circle for the best self-published book of 2007. Her novel, *Embracing Change,* won First Place in the Rose & Crown New Novels Competition of 2009. She entered the first chapter of Magnitude 7.1 & 6.3 in the Faithwriter's "Page Turner" Competition in 2010 and was awarded second place. Debbie's writing has also opened doors for public speaking and she is often asked to share her life story and her experiences as a writer.

www.debbieroome.com
debbieroome@gmail.com

Books by Debbie Roome

A collection of stories about the Canterbury earthquakes. More than 40 men, women and children share experiences that will shock, amaze and inspire. Includes black and white photos and a firsthand account of the 1929 Murchison earthquake.

Inspirational romance that took first place in the 2009 Rose & Crown novel-writing competition in the UK. This heart-warming story is set in New Zealand and South Africa and has a strong theme of hope and forgiveness.

Lindsay's life in Christchurch is turned upside down when Mind Games and evidence drag her into a murder case – as a suspect. Kindle Version only.

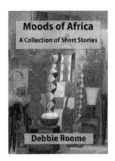

Moods of Africa is a collection of inspirational short stories set in various parts of Africa. These stories have a Christian theme and are sure to tug on your heart strings. Kindle version only.

Tender Christmas Tales is a collection of short Christmas stories with a Christian theme. Read about the dying girl who held the hands of two fathers and the unborn baby who received his first Christmas gift from his mother. Kindle version only.

Made in the USA
Charleston, SC
04 October 2012